Regional Economic Integration in East Asia

This interdisciplinary book analyses the regional economic integration and its institutionalisation that has been pursued in East Asia since the late 1990s and its far-reaching impact for the entire region and beyond.

It presents the specificity and evolution of East Asia's economic integration as well as its outcomes in the form of an impressive number of free trade agreements concluded by East Asian countries. The book also addresses the region's institutionalised regionalism of the 21st century, embodied by the recent establishment of two mega-regional institutions for trade and investment facilitation – Comprehensive and Progressive Agreement for Trans-Pacific Partnership and Regional Comprehensive Economic Partnership, analysing their economic potential and impact on East Asian economies as well as on regions, including Europe. Additionally, the book offers a comprehensive analysis of integration theories, providing political and economic theories of integration and related conceptual discussions, which may help understand the uniqueness of the East Asian model of integration.

The book will be useful for students and researchers in economics, international relations and political science, as well as government administrations and private businesses developing long-term strategic plans towards the region of East Asia.

Magdalena Suska is an Assistant Professor at SGH Warsaw School of Economics, Poland.

Routledge Focus on Economics and Finance

The fields of economics are constantly expanding and evolving. This growth presents challenges for readers trying to keep up with the latest important insights. Routledge Focus on Economics and Finance presents short books on the latest big topics, linking in with the most cutting-edge economics research.

Individually, each title in the series provides coverage of a key academic topic, whilst collectively the series forms a comprehensive collection across the whole spectrum of economics.

Customer Data Sharing Frameworks
Twelve Lessons for the World
Anton Didenko, Natalia Jevglevskaja and Ross P. Buckley

Crowdfunding European Business
Antonella Francesca Cicchiello

The Chief Financial Officer and Corporate Performance
Finance, Governance and Risk
Elżbieta Bukalska, Anna Wawryszuk-Misztal and Tomasz Sosnowski

Artists Labour Market, Cultural Policy and Creative Economy
A Triangular Model in Poland
Dorota Ilczuk, Anna Karpińska and Emilia Cholewicka

Reading John Maynard Keynes
A Short Introduction
Andrés Solimano

Regional Economic Integration in East Asia
Institutions, Agreements and the European Experience
Magdalena Suska

For more information about this series, please visit: www.routledge.com/Routledge-Focus-on-Economics-and-Finance/book-series/RFEF

Regional Economic Integration in East Asia

Institutions, Agreements and the European Experience

Magdalena Suska

Routledge
Taylor & Francis Group
LONDON AND NEW YORK

First published 2025
by Routledge
4 Park Square, Milton Park, Abingdon, Oxon OX14 4RN

and by Routledge
605 Third Avenue, New York, NY 10158

Routledge is an imprint of the Taylor & Francis Group, an informa business

British Library Cataloguing-in-Publication Data
A catalogue record for this book is available from the British Library

Library of Congress Cataloging-in-Publication Data
Names: Suska, Magdalena, author.
Title: Regional economic integration in East Asia : institutions, agreements and the European experience / Magdalena Suska.
Description: Abingdon, Oxon ; New York, NY : Routledge, 2025. |
Series: Routledge focus on economics and finance | Includes bibliographical references and index.
Identifiers: LCCN 2024036976 (print) | LCCN 2024036977 (ebook) | ISBN 9781032897103 (hardback) | ISBN 9781032897134 (paperback) | ISBN 9781003544234 (ebook)
Subjects: LCSH: East Asia—Economic integration. | Regionalism—East Asia.
Classification: LCC HC460.5 .S876 2025 (print) | LCC HC460.5 (ebook) | DDC 338/.064095—dc23/eng/20240904
LC record available at https://lccn.loc.gov/2024036976
LC ebook record available at https://lccn.loc.gov/2024036977

ISBN: 9781032897103 (hbk)
ISBN: 9781032897134 (pbk)
ISBN: 9781003544234 (ebk)

DOI: 10.4324/9781003544234

Typeset in Times New Roman
by codeMantra

Contents

Figures

Tables

About the author

Magdalena Suska, PhD in Political Science, is an Assistant Professor at SGH Warsaw School of Economics. She has MAs in International Economic and Political Relations from the SGH Warsaw School of Economics and in English Philology from Warsaw University. She lectures in the field of Global Business and International Management. She has been engaged in numerous international projects promoting Polish doctoral students and academic teachers as well as Polish businesses on global markets. Her research interests include international economics and management, including economic integration, international trade, models of economic growth, sustainable development and Corporate Social Responsibility (CSR). She is the author of scientific publications in the field of economics and political science.

Introduction

East Asia is one of the world's most dynamic and fastest growing regions, which embraces some of the largest and most prosperous economies, including China, Hong Kong, Taiwan, Japan and South Korea. East Asia's spectacular growth is largely attributed to the favourable environment for the development of industry and trade, along with natural resource abundance and surplus labour force of relatively low-cost and adaptable workers. A swift adjustment to the requirements of new technologies as well as exceptional work discipline and ethics demonstrated by East Asian nations is, certainly, not without significance.

However, East Asia lags behind other regions when it comes to economic integration, especially in comparison to Europe. For latecomer countries, economic development and integration is one, inseparable issue regulated by national governments rather than left to private actors and business sector. In East Asia, this development–integration relationship took a different form than the traditional approach. East Asia's economic growth was fuelled by East Asian countries, participating in dynamic production networks spanned by private enterprises. These phenomena were accompanied by increased regional competition for export markets and foreign direct investment, which, in turn, prompted East Asian economies to introduce voluntary trade and investment liberalisation. Together with growing importance of East Asian markets, the character of regional relations and processes ongoing in the region has changed. East Asia, leading in market-driven integration processes, with deepening intra-regional trade and investment ties in the absence of a formal, institutional framework for cooperation, has been evolving towards the institutionalisation of regional economic integration. Especially, the 1997 Asian financial crisis envisaged the East Asian nations the necessity to institutionalise their regional cooperation to avoid future crises of that kind. It triggered a wave of structural reforms in the region and opened a new stage in regional economic policies and relations, based not only on "loose" regional fora, like Association of Southeast Asian Nations (ASEAN) and Asia-Pacific Economic Cooperation (APEC), but also on more formal mechanisms and institutions. It was first reflected by the rise of ASEAN Plus Three cooperation dialogue and post-crisis financial cooperative schemes (e.g., Chiang Mai Initiative and Chiang Mai Initiative Multilateralization), then by the rapid proliferation of free trade agreements (FTAs) in the region; ASEAN Economic Community, Comprehensive and Progressive Agreement for Trans-Pacific Partnership (CPTPP) and Regional Comprehensive Economic Partnership (RCEP) are probably the most important ones among them. So far, the latter is the culmination of a decades-long pursuit of trade liberalisation and market integration within the world's economically most dynamic and most important region. The establishment of CPTPP and RCEP is a milestone in the process of the institutionalisation of East Asia's economic integration and both mega-regional trading arrangements are currently shaping a new order of regional and region-wide cooperation, with great practical significance.

Although the region of East Asia still lags behind Europe in terms of regional integration, East Asian countries are catching up with the processes and their dynamics is visible. However, not only opportunities but also a number of threats connected to East Asia's economic integration can be seen, like, e.g., the "spaghetti effect" or rather the "noodle bowl" effect in the Asian reality. Also, economic, political and social inconsistencies are notable in East Asia. After three decades of rapid economic growth and development, huge income differences still exist in the region. The aforementioned phenomena have inclined the author to undertake exploratory studies on the integration theories and the institutionalisation process of economic integration ongoing among East Asian countries, embodied by the creation of two mega-regional trade agreements – RCEP and CPTPP – and their economic effects on the region. Additionally, recognising East Asia's economic and growth dynamics as well as growing significance of the entire region in international relations (including the economic and trade relations with Europe), it is also worth investigating their potential impact on Europe and the European Union (EU).

In the light of the considerations presented above, the main aim of this monography is to present regional economic integration and its institutionalisation on the example of East Asian countries and their implications from the European perspective. By doing so, the author strives to engage the reader not only in thinking critically about East Asian economic integration and the potential impact (opportunities and threat) of the recently established RCEP and CPTPP on regional trade architecture but also the European trade policy and strategy towards East Asia and the Asia-Pacific. Specifically, the author aims at systemising the knowledge about integration theories (political and economic theories) and conceptualising the terminology, i.e., economic integration and related terms as well as institutions and institutionalisation and embedding them in the new theory of institutional economics to proceed to the analysis of the specificity and character of East Asian economic integration and its evolution towards institutionalised regionalism. Through these analyses, the author makes an attempt to anchor East Asia's regional integration in the theory of economics and show its uniqueness and distinctive character from other models of regional integration, especially the European integration. Moreover, the author strives for presenting the outcomes of institutionalisation processes embodied in the establishment of regional and region-wide FTAs, with a special emphasis on two regional institutional arrangements to facilitate trade (and investment) – RCEP and CPTPP – to assess their current and potential impact not only on regional trade but also on trade with the third countries, especially the EU.

The above-mentioned aims of this monography have been supplemented by the following research questions, which are addressed in the subsequent chapters:

- How have integration theories evolved and what are their assumptions?
- What are the characteristics of East Asian pattern of integration and how does it differ from the European model of integration? How did the evolutionary process of its institutionalisation proceed?
- What was the role of multinational enterprises in East Asian integration processes?
- What was the function of ASEAN and APEC in institutionalising economic integration in East Asia?
- What does East Asian trade architecture look like? What regional trade institutions have been created as a result of ongoing institutionalisation processes in East Asia and what are their specific features?
- What are the attributes and significance of CPTPP and RCEP for the regional trade architecture? What are the actual and potential economic effects of both regional institutional arrangements?
- What are the opportunities and risks of CPTPP and RCEP for Europe and the EU and what are the implications for its trade policy strategy towards the region of East Asia and the Asia-Pacific?

In order to maintain the logical sequence of the analysis as well as to retain the theoretical, empirical and implicative character of the study, the monography is divided into four chapters, preceded by introduction and proceeded by conclusions and implications for the economic policy. The specificity and topic of the monography have determined the research methods, which include literature reviews, descriptive and comparative analyses as well as statistical method.

1 The theory of integration

Integration in a political sense and political integration are related to social sciences in a broader sense, whereas narrowly related to political and economic sciences. The meaning of integration in a political sense could be identified with "uniting", "unifying" or "organizing in a group of two or more units". On the other hand, it reflects "centralisation" (Hoppe, 2007, p. 109). Hence, integration in political sense, perceived as uniting and centralisation, which results in building a political community by political units, is connected to several elements, like, among others, establishing the unified frame of rules and regulations, creating common institutions with decision-making power and projecting the identity of the integrated community. The core of this integrating activity is the process of delegating the autonomy of political units to the newly formed political community. Integration in a political sense embraces various forms and interpretations. In a broader sense, we can distinguish between two (corresponding to each other) categories of integration, namely political and economic integration as well as regional and global integration. The first category is based on a sector variable, whereas the criterion of the second one is geography. The monography emphasises both categories of the broader meaning of integration in a political sense – economic integration and regional integration. However, in order to proceed to theorise on integration processes in the economic dimension, it is necessary, first, to revise the theory of political integration. Hence, this chapter is structured according to three parts. First, selected political theories of integration are discussed (which are, in fact, also related to economic integration), i.e., the theory of pluralism, federalism, functionalism, neofunctionalism and liberal intergovernmentalism. Then the author presents traditional and new economic integration theories to finally proceed to the analysis of the economic integration theory for developing countries.

1.1 Political theories of integration

The first theories of integration in a political sense have their roots in the theories of social contract. In that sense, the social contract could be identified

DOI: 10.4324/9781003544234-1

with integration, but on individual level. The subjects of the integration were the individuals, which limited their freedom in favour of the newly established political community. This kind of integration was researched by several philosophers, such as Hobbes, Locke and Rousseau. At the same period, Kant went one step further and provided the basis for global integration in a political sense. The author proposed the idea of global federation that consists of republics that delegate their sovereignty to upper state level and achieve a global integration in a political sense (Kant, 1917). However, under the concept of integration in a political sense, various forms and interpretations of integration can be found. This part of the monography focuses on the explanation of the integration process within the category of political integration, referring to the theory of pluralism, federalism, functionalism and neofunctionalism as well as modern mainstreams in political science theories, including the fusion thesis and liberal intergovernmentalism.

1.1.1 Pluralism

Starting the considerations on the theory of pluralism from the meaning of the term, it is noted that "pluralism" is often used as a synonym of "diversity". Dahl (1978, p. 191) used this term in two different, although related, ways, distinguishing between conflictive pluralism and organisational pluralism. The first refers to "the number and pattern of relatively enduring cleavages that must be taken into account in order to characterize conflicts among a given collection of persons", whereas the latter is associated with "the number and the autonomy of organisations that must be taken into account in order to characterise conflicts among a given collection of persons". According to the author, organisational pluralism is the greater, the greater the number of organisations is, and the greater their autonomy is. Dahl further claimed that political systems, allowing for a significant measure of autonomy to important units, are referred to as pluralistic, and the extent of their pluralism is dependent on four interrelated factors: (1) the amount of latent conflictive pluralism; (2) the nature of the socioeconomic order; (3) the nature of the political regime; and (4) the concrete structure of the political institutions.

According to the assumptions of the theory of pluralism, represented, among others, by Deutsch, Puchala, Kaplan, Alker, Plischke and Inglehart, a national state is a fundamental subject of international relations (IR). Thus, the process of integration refers to the creation of the community of states, whose basic values are sovereignty as well as international peace and security. One of the foremost authors of pluralism, Deutsch (2003, pp. 122–124), maintained that the principal problem of each civilisation that wishes to survive is finding an appropriate form of cooperation to eliminate "war as a social institution". The author further emphasised that the main aim and task faced by integrating states is the creation of such a community, which would be, in essence, a "security-community", defined as the one in which there is real assurance that its members will not fight each other physically but will settle their disputes in some other way. If the entire world were integrated as a security-community, wars would be automatically eliminated. Deutsch (2003, p. 124) introduced two types of the security-community, dividing it into an amalgamated and pluralistic one. The former is a merger of two or more previously independent units into a single larger unit, with a unitary or federal government, whereas the latter retains "the legal independence of separate governments", with two supreme decision-making centres.

Deutsch (1953, 1954, 1963, 1964) elaborated a specific model of political integration based on a socio-casual paradigm (developed later by Puchala, 1966, Alker and Puchala, 1968), which embraces three elements. First, an integrated political community must possess certain structural components. Namely, a certain form of supranational institutions must exist, which have the power to make binding and authoritative decisions for the community. The second element of an integrated political community is the existence of a certain political process. Because of the fact that supranational institutions have the power of decision-making, the political elites of the community will focus their demands on community institutions. Moreover, the actors involved in presenting demands to community institutions should not be national governments, but rather transnational interest groups. An additional characteristic of the political process is the absence of national violence. The third element of the integrated political community is the existence of a transnational society – a population in which there is exposure to common experience and social heritage, as well as similar preferences, expectations and aspirations. Under such conditions, the society will support the common set of institutions and non-violent style of political decision-making.

Hence, it can be concluded that, according to the theory of pluralism, integration occurs at three levels: (1) the intergovernmental–diplomatic level; (2) the social level and (3) the level of an individual person. The main aim of so understood political integration is establishing an international system of national states, which reflects a high degree of communication, in the absence of supranational institutions. The solution is to develop such a form of cooperation that gives the sense of partnership, simultaneously excluding war as a way of resolving disputes among states. Therefore, the process of communicating and the ability to exchange information are extremely important for all types of coordination and cooperation. Hence, pluralism emphasises, in the first place, contacts, exchange and communication among people – so called social-communication concept of integration. Thus, the three notions "the pluralistic theory" as well as "the theory of communication" and "transactionism" are used interchangeably.[1]

Other factors, equally important for integration, embrace geographical channels of communication, people's mobility, the multiplicity and equilibrium of mutual transactions, the exchange of roles within groups as well as predictability of reciprocal behaviours (Deutsch, 1954). While examining the above-mentioned parameters, the flow of goods and services, people, information as well as symbols among states can be determined; thus, the probability of their integration can be assessed.

Deutsch (1954, p. 129) and Pentland (1973, p. 48) also emphasised the psychological dimension of identity at the level of an individual; hence, all changes in the behaviour of individuals can have an impact on the community of states. The notions such as "sense of community", "we feeling", trust, mutual consideration and perception of needs accentuated the psychological and social dimension of integration. In this sense the community would be connected to the possibility of communicating, and the flow of information will reflect the coherence of the organisation. Additionally, in this context, Deutsch (1954, p. 130) introduced the notion of "social learning", which plays a significant role in acquiring the habits of political behaviour, indispensable during the creation of the sense of community. People learn these habits

> in the face of background conditions which change only slowly, so that they appear at any moment as something given – as political, economic, social or psychological facts that must be taken for granted for the purposes of short-range politics. The speed and extent of this learning of habits of integrative political behaviour are influenced by (…) the particular movement toward integration.
>
> (Deutsch, 1953, p. 91)

Both the society and community develop in a process of social learning; community, in turn, comprises of people, who learn how to communicate and understand each other to a higher degree than it is needed for a simple exchange of goods and services.

Summing up the considerations presented above, the respect for international peace and national security together with the policy of strategic diplomatic actions as well as the conviction that the state is a foundation for political life are the main assumptions of the pluralistic concept of integration. The security community perceived as an integrated group of states reinforces the international stability due to national diversity, autonomy and sovereignty. The cooperation among integrating states is based on the increased exchange of information, which, in turn, reinforces the sense of common interest, values and benefits resulting from integration.

Some theorists criticise several assumptions of pluralism, perceiving the flow of information and transactions as the partial evidence of the community's existence and not its cause (Alker and Puchala, 1968). Haas (1964) indicated the fact that the parameters, which are used by pluralists as a measure of the level of integration, can be simultaneously applied to determine this process. Consequently, it is difficult to define what is a cause and what is an effect (e.g., if a high degree of trade exchange between two countries is an integrating factor or the evidence that integration has already occurred). Whereas, according to Pentland (1973), the pluralistic concept is appropriate to describe integration, it has a relatively low explicatory and prediction attribute, which is expected from each reliable scientific theory. In turn, Lindberg (1967, p. 345) referring to the category of "community", "we feeling" and "mutual consideration" claimed that Deutsch developed not the political integration theory, but rather a concept of a "social and moral community", which omits numerous facts of political significance.

1.1.2 Federalism

While in the pluralistic theory two indications of integration are brought to the forefront of considerations – the primacy of international peace and national security and self-driving policy of strategic diplomatic actions as an example of cooperation among nations – federalists postulate the creation of federation and a federal system of government.[2] The term "federation" and thereby "federalism" originates from the Latin word – *foedus* and means covenant, contract or pact. Such covenants were concluded in ancient Rome between the allied states or *foederati*. The act of forming such a covenant was rooted in the key principles of equity, partnership, reciprocity, toleration and respect. Davis (1978) pointed out to the term *fides* (meaning faith and trust) and to the fact that covenantal federalism evolved over the years to refer to a voluntary union of different actors, i.e., people, communities or states.

However, it should be here emphasised that federalists, while referring to the above-mentioned principles, mean a form of association, i.e., a union, but not a unity. One of the fundamental functions of federalism focuses on establishing a clear vertical dividing line between the authority and responsibility within the particular levels of the country's governing. Such a system aims at the integration of heterogenous organisms while retaining their autonomy, and the main objective of the established political union is respecting unity in diversity. In other words, the purpose of the federal union is to integrate different entities, but not to assimilate them. Hence it is a union, but of a specific type. It has "two faces": it is both a unifying force and a means to maintain "difference and diversity" (Burges, 2009, p. 29). As a consequence, a federal union is associated with both the process of political unification among sovereign states, i.e., the establishment of a single state by aggregation – a federation, in which central and local governments cooperate with each other (the process of integration) and retaining independence and the diffusion of power (the process of disintegration).

Kinskey (1979) distinguished four different approaches to the interpretation of federalism. First, it may describe the theory of integration, i.e., a model of maintaining peaceful relations among states. One of the examples of such a perception of federalism is Churchill's speech of 1949 about the need to create the United States of Europe. Second, federalism can be interpreted as a theory of decentralisation. However, this interpretation contradicts the idea of an absolute and centralised state. Instead, it promotes a certain social model reflecting an active participation of individuals/citizens in the political life. Moreover, perceiving federalism in a broader perspective as systemic principles of the state, it promulgates the respect for pluralistic society based on the subsidiarity principle, which refers to the German social and political thought of the 19th and 20th centuries. Finally, we can distinguish so called "integral federalism", which results from the human nature. Such a philosophical and ideological approach originates from the concept of personalism in the 1920s and 1930s of the 20th century, according to which a human functions in the society while interacting with other people, and at the same time becomes responsible for shaping this society.

In turn, Dosenrode (2018) perceived federalism through the prism of two theories – a politico-ideological theory of action and an academic theory of regional integration. The first theory is of political rather than academic interest, whereas the second one, following the common practice in IR theory, is divided into two categories – liberal and realist theory.[3] The author believes that federalism, as a theory of regional integration, was abandoned too early since, among others, it had been connected to the development of the European Community (EU), which was in crisis from the mid-1970s till the mid-1980s.

Federalism, in the context of the European Union (EU), is understood as the "application of federal principles to the process of European integration, where the term integration refers to the sense of a coming together of previously separate or independent parts to form a new whole" (Burgess, 2009, p. 30). In this sense, two main visions (strands) of federalism after World War II can be distinguished, which were represented by Monnet and by Spinelli.[4] The difference between these two approaches was that according to Monnet, the ultimate goal of political integration was implicit, and it should be realised through gradual integration. Spinelli, in turn, wished Europe to become federalised as soon as possible. Monnet believed in the "political strategy of small concrete, economic steps, which would culminate in a federal Europe". In contrast, Spinelli supported the radical strategy of "starting with the political institutions and a popularly endorsed treaty that would be quickly translated into the familiar statist language of a constitution" (Burges, 2009, p. 32). In addition to Monnet's "federalism by instalments" and Spinelli's "democratic radicalism", Burgess (2009) and Roemheld (1990) also distinguish a third strand of federalism referred to as "integral", "personalist" or "Proudhonian" federalism, which embraces a wide range of political and sociological ideas based on the notion of European society and the dissemination of federalist principles and values across the delimited boundaries of European states. The discussed above three strands of federalism emphasise the rich tradition of philosophical, ideological and empirical ideas and strategies that have been elaborated in response to the phenomenon of the integrating European countries.

It should be emphasised that in the mainstream literature two terms are distinguished – federalism and federation. The former is identified as the original and driving force of the latter. Although there is a common consensus that federalism leads to federation, i.e., the establishment of a federation, a debate revolves around its nature – whether it is of a normative, prescriptive nature or it simply describes the emergence of a federation (Dosenrode, 2010). Federalism can be constructed as political ideology/philosophy, comprising a range of diverse interests and identities that are arranged around different historical, cultural, social and economic, ideological and philosophical factors, which are, in fact, original reasons that stand behind a federation. Federation, in turn, can be understood as an "institutional agreement, taking the form of a sovereign state and distinguished from other states solely by the fact that its central government incorporates regional units in its decision procedure on some constitutionally entrenched basis" (King, 1982, p. 77).

This distinction between the two above-mentioned notions is based on the way how the concept of federalism is realised, either bottom up or top-down. The first approach (i.e., moderate or evolutionary federalism) is based on the conclusion of a federal agreement among national governments to establish gradually a common political system, in which federalism is not a tool, but a result of establishing a new organism. Moderate federalists undermine the maintenance of state sovereignty, perceiving nationalism as a factor impeding the development of international cooperation. According to them, integration is a distinctive capability of a system to function in the face of internal and external factors. They also assume a self-driving process of integration (like functionalists), embracing new areas of cooperation, which, however, should begin from the sphere of economics. In moderate federalism, the need to establish appropriate institutions is also emphasised. In turn, according to the top-down approach (radical or revolutionary federalism), the establishment of a European federation is recommended, which exercises supranational power by means of a constitutional assembly emerged in common democratic elections or appointed by legislative bodies of states. Thus, federation is not a remote objective of integration, but a starting point. Its ultimate aim is to develop and implement a federal constitution, which would ensure the possibility of conducting an effective policy by the federal government. Radical federalists saw little chance in establishing the federation of West Europe; hence, they postulated the necessity to diminish the state sovereignty by appointing a great number of democratic supranational institutions equipped with certain autonomy (see, e.g., Mally, 1973, Miklaszewski, 1984, 1991).

1.1.3 Functionalism

The foremost functionalists, Mitrany (1943, 1966, 1975) and Sewell (1966), referred to two important ideas in the theory of functionalism – the durability of the community and benefits from its creation on the basis of a functional activity. One such benefit is peace. The experience of the World War II showed that the attempts to peacefully settle the relations among states failed; hence, functionalists envisaged the solution in the creation of an international community, which would prevent conflicts. Mitrany (1943, p. 92) believed that functionalism would yield "a new sense of peace: not a peace that would keep the nations quietly apart but a peace that would bring them actively together, not the old static and strategic view but a social view of peace". The author was interested in international cooperation for the sake of peace and a better life, thus creating conditions to avoid devastating conflicts among states over money and dominance, which result in wars. The implementation of these ideas requires the creation of an international community – the security community, which is based on the respect for common values and a belief in the possibility of peaceful conflict resolution.

Functionalist, in their views, referred to the concepts of federalists and pluralists. For example, Mitrany (1943, p. 152–153) argued that

> federation has indeed merely created a new a larger political unit which in the process did bring peace within the group, but it has not been proved that its creation necessarily contributed also to peace between it and other groups. The prospects of two powerful federations (…) facing each other across Europe, is not a comforting one.

Deutsch et al. (1968) claimed that functionalism succeeds under less favourable conditions than are required for the success of federations. Moreover, functional communities survive more unfavourable processes that might destroy federations. Etzioni (1965) illustrated the weaknesses of a federation vs. functionalism on the example of the United Arab Republic (UAR) (1958–1961) and the Federation of the West Indies (1962–1965). The author envisaged the failure of the UAR in the fact that it "was born prematurely and the integrating power was in constant decline, especially in the last year of the union" (Etzioni, 1965, p. 97). In turn, the Federation of the West Indies failed because of the attempt by an external power (Britain) to make the idea of federation more acceptable to a greater number of islands in the region by reducing the scope of the proposed federation. However, this did not leave the new federation with a substantial base on which to grow, develop and serve interest of its leading members.

In functionalism, the concept of integration is based on several assumptions. First, it emphasises the need to gradual learning of the mutual cooperation among states, which conditions the development of Deutsch's "we feeling" in the sphere of interests, identity and sovereignty. Functionalists attach particular importance to the sense of a psychological community (of people and social groups) rather than the community in a legal–institutional form.

Second, the integration process may be described using the phenomenon of "spill-over", which means that initiating the cooperation in one field creates the demand for the cooperation in other areas. Thus, we can speak about certain "self-driving" of integration. On the spill-over effect, Monnet's vision of integration was based, who believed that creating integrating ties in the sector of coal and steel under the European Coal and Steel Community (ECSC) would enable further development of integration in other sectors.

Third, functionalists put emphasis on economic integration. Because of the fact that the potential for cooperation is the greatest in the economic sphere, this is the economy from which integration should be started. Mitrany (1943) stressed that political elements should be separated from the economic spheres of cooperation and act as a self-driving function of economic integration.

Moreover, the functionalist theory assumes that cooperation among states cannot be realised on the basis of traditional functions of a state. Instead, it is necessary to gradually delegate certain tasks of a state to an international institution. As a result of tightening international ties, state attributes will slowly disappear, and full integration will be achieved. The transfer of sovereignty to functional international institutions requires the establishment of a psychological community consisting of citizens who will be loyal to these institutions and believe that they will effectively satisfy their social and economic needs. Functionalists opt more for global cooperation rather than regional, suggesting the creation of international institutions/agencies, which would take over the functions of states. Mitrany (1943, p. 105) pointed out that many activities in the past had been "organised internationally by private agencies – in finance and trade and production, etc., not to speak of scientific and cultural activities". Hence, the author anticipated a growth of functional institutions, such as economic, social and technical agencies within the United Nations. Sewell (1966), in turn, envisaged the active role of the International Bank for Reconstruction and Development and its affiliate, the International Development Association, in providing economic assistance to developing nations. Nevertheless, it should be emphasised that functionalists generally put an emphasis on the practice of integration rather than the process of institutionalisation.

Furthermore, functionalism also assumes the need to perceive integration from a static (as a process, a system of changes) or dynamic (as a state of affairs, a system of maintenance) perspective. Hence, two approaches to functionalism can be distinguished: (1) sociological functionalism, focused on the system of maintenance and (2) international functionalism, related to the system of changes. Sociological functionalism emphasises supplying goods as the initial aim of the economy, which is a sub-system providing the material foundations of welfare, whereas the political sub-sub-system (the authority) uses these means (material goods) to fulfil common aims. In turn, international functionalism perceives integration as a process of numerous interactions and growing national ties. All actions taken should be oriented to the fulfilment of the aim, which is integration, and its realisation will be possible due to the creation of an open system of reciprocal compromises. The process of integration interpreted from dynamic perspective depends on the capacities of national governments to adjust to the needs of the integrating community and on the development of such solutions that would take into consideration the interests of its participants. International functionalism distances itself from ideological tendencies and clearly communicates the apolitical character of IR; hence, the development of international cooperation, leading to economic integration, takes place outside the existing political arrangement.

1.1.4 Neofunctionalism

The acquis of functionalism has been developed by neofunctionalism, which belongs to the theories of regional integration. This theory was first formulated in the late 1950s and early 1960s, preliminary through the work of Haas (1958, 1960, 1961 1964a, 1964b, 1967, 1970, 1976, 2001, 2004) and Lindberg (1963) in response to the establishment of the ECSC and the European Economic Community (EEC). The original neofunctionalist theory was later developed by, among others, Lindberg and Scheingold (1970, 1971), Nye (1965, 1971), Puchala (1972), Schmitter (1969, 1970, 1971, 1996, 1997, 2004) and Niemann and Schmitter (2009).

The most flourishing period of the neofunctionalist theory was until the mid-1960s, during which period the evolution of European integration[5] seemed to confirm its assumptions. From the mid-1960s, the theory was, however, increasingly criticised, which culminated during the Empty Chair crisis of 1965–1966, when the French President Charles de Gaulle seriously weakened the operations of the EEC. Nevertheless, in the late 1960s and early 1970s, and then with the resurgence of the process of European integration in the mid-1980s, neofunctionalists made an attempt to revise the fundamental assumptions of the concept and incorporate it into newer mainstreams of the theory of integration.

Neofunctionalism finds its intellectual roots at the juncture between functionalist, federalist and communications theories, but it also indirectly refers to the "group theorists" of American politics. In the neofunctionalist theory, Haas and Lindberg combined functionalist mechanisms with federalist objectives. Similar to functionalism, neofunctionalism accentuates the mechanism of technocratic decision-making, incremental change and learning processes. However, regarding several assumptions, it clearly departs from Mitrany's functionalism. For example, while functionalism assumes that the type and purpose of an organisation is determined by the task it is supposed to fulfil, neofunctionalism emphasises the autonomous impact of supranational institutions and the emerging role of organised interests. Functionalism does not limit integration to any territorial area, whereas in neofunctionalism, the global approach to integration is considered to be inappropriate and is given a specifically regional focus. Neofunctionalists also present a different approach to peace than power or law as proposed by functionalists and pluralists. As Haas (1958, p. xiv) argued, "states, instead of struggling for power, are expected to defend their preferences and to cooperate when cooperation is deemed necessary for their realisation".

In neofunctionalism, several assumptions encapsulate the driving forces of the process of political integration. First, the presence of rational, interest-driven national and supranational elites (but not masses of people), recognising the limitations of national solutions, is assumed. Neofunctionalists perceive the community as a "creature of elites", which act at the supranational level – it seeks supranational solutions to its problems and possibilities to report their demands to supranational institutions (Haas, 1958; Lindberg, 1963). It means, in practice, that elites and interest groups (formed mainly by the economic sector – entrepreneurs, professional associations, trade unions) shift their expectations, loyalties and activities towards supranational institutions, which are primarily motivated by these actors' interests. Simultaneously, their attitude is changing during the integration process, as they learn from the benefits of regional policies and their experience in cooperative decision-making (Haas, 1958, p. 291; Niemann and Schmitter, 2009, p. 48). Thus, they are encouraged to establish a common position, and the role of consensus, i.e., searching for a compromise to realise their own interests, is increasing. As far as these interests do not have to be compatible, an institutional framework is established to provide a common platform for the activities performed by political elites.

Second, the key engine for the development of integration is also institutional structures and the transfer of decision-making from national governments to supranational institutions. Regional integration takes place, when social actors, considering their own interests, decide to rely on supranational institutions rather than their own governments to fulfil their demands, which, in turn, gain increasing authority and legitimacy. In other words, the progress of integration leads to broadening the competences of the community's institutions. For example, as a result of European integration, a political system based on "multilevel governance" was created, in which decisions are taken partially by supranational institutions and partially by national governments. Haas (1958, p. xvi), however, argued that neofunctionalism downplays the national governments "in the interest of puffing up supranational organisations".

Third, the behaviour pattern of elites in the integration process is a source of a new political system, requiring a specific decision-making style and the combination of institutional structures at the national and the community level. Among various styles of decision-making, we can distinguish between purely political and more economic choices with hidden political implications in line with the politics of common markets. If the aims of politicians and elites are purely political, regional integration either proceeds directly and smoothly or it is impossible. However, when their objectives are incrementally oriented towards economic aspects, integration goes forward gradually, but automatically. However, as Haas (1970, p. 627) pointed out, most political actors are incapable of engaging in long-term purposive behaviour as they "stumble" from one decision to the other one. Additionally, these decisions are usually taken with highly imperfect knowledge of their consequences and frequently under the pressure of deadlines.

Finally, neofunctionalists emphasised the role of the theory of regional integration, which addresses different aspects of both economic and political integration. These two types of integration are connected to each other by the effect of spill-over. Haas initially believed that the spill-over process is automatic (or quasi automatic), and integration will proceed automatically as demands for additional central services intensify when central institutions prove incapable of meeting the demands of their new clients. Thus, activities of certain integrated sectors will "spill-over" into the neighbouring (not yet integrated) ones, but now becoming the focus of demands for more integration (Haas, 2004, p. xv). In other words, initial steps toward integration trigger endogenous economic and political dynamics leading to further cooperation.

In fact, neofunctionalists identify two types of spill-over effects – functional and political, which both deepen and widen integration by working through, among others, interest group pressure, public opinion and elite socialisation (George, 1985, 1994). The functional spill-over occurs, when incomplete integration undermines the effectiveness of existing policies in areas that are already integrated and in related sectors of the economy, thus, pressing on the expansion of policy coordination. The idea is that some sectors are so interdependent that it is impossible to isolate them from the rest. Therefore, integration in one sector at the regional level is only predictable in combination with integration of other sectors. Haas (1958, p. 297) argued that sector integration "begets its own impetus toward extension of the entire economy". For example, the viability of integration in the coal and steel sectors would be undermined unless other related industries, such as, e.g., the transportation sector, ensure a continued movement of necessary raw materials (Niemann and Schmitter, 2009). The functional spill-over is economic in nature and reflects the closely interlinked feature of modern economies, in which government intervention in one sector contributes to economic distortions in other areas. For example, as Caporaso and Keeler (1993) indicated, without continuously enhanced policy coordination, the EU would fail to cope with the complexity of issues (sometimes highly controversial) on the European agenda and thus would lose its legitimacy.

In turn, the political spill-over takes place when the existence of supranational organisations triggers the self-reinforcing process of institution-building. It results from the spill-over of economic functions and can be defined as a self-driven process of creating new common institutions and new spheres of integration. The engine for this process is the supranational authorities, which have a certain measure of autonomous, decision initiative and can drive by themselves the development of integration.

The theory of neofunctionalism has been widely used for the interpretation of European integration, especially in federalist mainstream combining the sphere of economic integration with the creation of political supranational structures. The theory emphasises the principle of gradual integration based on the "spill-over" principle and simultaneously creates the elements of the political theory allowing to incorporate institutional issues to the analysis of integration. It also stresses the role of supranational authorities, such as officials, judges, parliamentarians and workers of the European Commission, who are becoming the engine of European integration. For example, the latter "engineer integration" by articulating objectives, recruiting and organising officials, proposing new policies or brokering bargains (Lindberg and Scheingold, 1970; Pentland, 1973; George, 1994).

Neofunctionalism, after its peak of popularity during the mid-1960s, was increasingly criticised by intergovernmentalists as well as neofunctionalists themselves – not even mentioned the self-critiques of its founding father. Shortcomings of the original neofunctionalism became evident during the wave of globalisation of the 1970s and unpleasant experience in advanced societies associated to stagflation. Haas (2004) pointed out that these events, together with Eurosclerosis, implied that there was no automaticity and no reliable spill-over in the process of European integration.

In response to criticism, neofunctionalists made an effort to modify the theory of original neofunctionalism. For example, Stone et al. (2001) extended it by envisaging the continuum anchored in intergovernmental politics at one end and in supranational politics at the other. The authors introduced the core concepts of an "institution" and "institutionalisation", assuming the emergence of dense network of rules and organisations binding member governments, interest groups, bureaucracies and politicians in even tighter interdependencies.

It is worth noting here that initially institutions were not granted much attention in neofunctionalism until the pioneering studies on the theory of organisations by March et al. (1958) and Selznick (1959). Stone et al. (2001) reflected the renewed interest in institutionalism, expanding traditional social institutionalism, focused mainly on explaining the stability and equilibrium in collective behaviour, by seeking to understand change. Moreover, the authors extended the concept of the "spill-over" effect confined to economic sectors to cover the unintended growth of any kind of the EU institution, whether related to economic activity or not (e.g., administrative and judicial organs).

In turn, Schmitter (1971) rejected the automaticity of spill-over in the integration process. The author introduced the effects of "spill-back" and "spill-around" to show why integration based on the spill-over logic is far from automatic. Moreover, the author perceived the diving forces of regional integration not only in the endogenous factors, but also in the exogenous ones, regarding them not as an impediment but as a facilitator of integration. Schmitter (2004) also introduced a model of decision cycles to illustrate the dynamics of his modified approach to original neofunctionalism. The author claimed that the initiating cycles, through which the EU passed already long time ago, were followed by priming cycles that condition the changing dynamics of member states in-between decision cycles. He also argued that European integration did not reach the transforming cycle, when the potential for the functional integration of the EU's economies would be exhausted and the emphasis would be put on the integration of polities.

Summing up, it is worth noting that neofunctionalism puts an emphasis not only on social structures and the community of states, highlighted by functionalists, but also on the institutional arrangement and political organisation of integration. Consequently, neofunctionalism is closer to political theory, whereas functionalism – to sociology. Whereas functionalism pays greater attention to the change of the society's civic values, neofunctionalism stresses the role of political and functional spill-over. Neofunctionalism, however, despite the complexity of its insights, does not fully explain all the issues related to integration, including the problems of European integration (Hoffman, 1966; Hansen, 1997; Taylor, 1983; Keohane and Nye, 1975; Webb, 1983; Keohane and Hoffmann, 1991; Cornett and Caporaso, 1992). One of the reasons for that is the fact that neofunctionalism fails to predict both the trajectory and the process of the EU's evolution. The only prediction neofunctionalism made about the EU's trajectory over time was that the technocratic imperative would lead to a "gradual", "automatic" and "incremental" progression toward deeper integration (Haas, 1964; 1967; 1976; Moravcsik, 1993, pp. 475–476).

1.1.5 Modern mainstreams in political science theories

The modern theory of integration attempts to expand the acquis of neofunctionalism by new spheres, out of which two are of particular significance: the trajectory of the development of integration processes and intergovernmental cooperation as the element of European political organisation.

Original neofunctionalism assumes that integration processes are gradual and automatically driven by the mechanism of functional and political spill-over, which is associated with a linear progress towards a higher degree of regional integration and greater impact of supranational factors. Consequently, a question arises, whether the progress of integration is a constant movement towards establishing a federal union of states (federation)? If so, how periodical crises and changes in integration processes occurring in different periods can be explained? The modern theory makes an attempt to address these issues, formulating models/trajectories of integration dynamics. One of these models is the Wessel's (1997) fusion thesis – an approach that provides a conceptual explanation of the course of EU integration and the perceptions and adjustment of the contributing political elites of member states.

The fusion thesis assumes that EU integration is the "logical product" of important choices made by EU governments. Member states agree to invest their competencies and allocate their resources in the EU due to "package deals" (Wessel, 1997, p. 274). In the process of EU integration, Rometsch and

Wessels (1996) distinguished three steps. The first step is Europeanisation, understood as the permeation of the supranational into the national and the sub-national. It contributes to a growing number of national actors participating in the EU political sphere, blurring the borders between the EU and national areas. The second step after Europeanisation towards integration is national fusion. It implies the growing reciprocity of influence between supranational and national institutions, which ultimately leads to an increase of exchanges between various levels of governance and increased sharing of responsibilities. The last step, which is the most integrative part of the process, is convergence. It is described as the "gradual process of institutional, procedural, and behavioural innovations and adaptations to the EU decision-making by national institutions" (Rometsch and Wessels, 1996, p. 236). As a result of the fusion, exchanges between member states and the EU institutions will intensify, leading to an increased interdependence among various actors at different levels. Moreover, there can be observed an increase in cooperation; consequently, national and supranational levels of governance cannot operate alone anymore. Hence, in the light of growing dependencies, member states need shared "problem-solving instruments" embodied by the EU supranational institutions (Wessel, 1997, pp. 273–274). According to the fusion thesis, due to variables such as interdependence, cooperation and growing reciprocal exchanges, national institutions are expected to share responsibilities horizontally (among states), vertically (with supranational institutions) and with other institutional bodies outside their sphere of control. Additionally, Wessels (2005, p. 27) envisaged not only a merger of public resources but also of legitimacy and other integrative instruments, which will allow member states to proceed towards greater convergence.

The second mainstream of the modern thought of integration, liberal intergovernmentalism, puts an emphasis on the element of confederation, connected to various forms of intragovernmental cooperation. It refers to the idea of neofunctionalism about the significance of international bargains for the dynamics of integration, thus, referring to the assumptions that the European system requires constant compromises and negotiations among member states or mediations within supranational institutions. However, the emphasis is put on the phenomenon, rather neglected by neofunctionalists, of shaping national preferences. Liberal intergovernmentalists argue that the theory of integration should not omit the specificity and differentiation of national preferences, showing the attitude of individual states to integration, in other words, determining the "demand" for integration. Moravcsik (1993) distinguished three significant elements constituting the core of liberal intergovernmentalism: (1) the assumption of rational state behaviour; (2) a liberal theory of national preference formation and (3) an intergovernmentalist analysis of interstate negotiations. States are actors that achieve their goals through intergovernmental negotiation and bargaining, rather than through centralised authority, making and enforcing political decisions. They take decisions to cooperate internationally in a three-stage framework: first states define preferences, then bargain to substantive agreements and finally create (or adjust) institutions to secure these outcomes (Moravcsik and Schimmelfenning, 2009).

Each country has a certain system of creating national preferences, as well as a mechanism of securing these preferences in the process of international cooperation. National preferences emerge as the result of operations of different national social and political groups and are articulated by a national government towards external partners during the negotiation and cooperation process. They are neither fixed, nor uniform; they vary among particular states, but also within the same state across time and addressed issues (Moravcsik, 2008).

Thus, to explain the outcomes of international negotiations among states with different national preferences, a bargaining theory of international cooperation is deployed. According to this theory, they depend on the actors' relative bargaining power, which may result from numerous factors, like, e.g., alternative policies and coalition, level and symmetry of information, extent of communication, institutional setting, possibility of making credible commitments, reputation, cost-effectiveness of threats and side-payments, relative preferences, risk acceptance and skills of the negotiating parties (Moravcsik, 1993). The efficiency of bargaining and the distribution of gains from cooperation among states reflect their relative power based on "asymmetrical independence" – those who gain the most economically from integration, relative to unilateral and collective alternatives, comprise the most on the margin to realise gains, whereas those who gain least tend to enjoy more clout to impose conditions (Moravcsik, 1998, p. 3).

Due to the fact that European cooperation means an eminent confrontation with the preferences of member states, an important task of integration is the creation of institutional framework, enabling intergovernmental bargains and coordination of national operations. As Moravcsik and Schimmelfenning (2009) pointed out, international institutions are instruments, which cope with unintended and often unwanted consequences. In line with the theory of neofunctionalism, states deliberately delegate authority to supranational institutions, which are capable of acting against the subsequent preferences of national governments and incorporate unintended and unwanted consequences under conditions of uncertainty (Keohane, 1984; Pierson, 1996; Fligstein, Stone and Sweet, 2001). Moravcsik and Schimmelfenning (2009) conclude that institutions enable states to reach a collectively superior outcome by reducing the transaction costs of further international negotiations on specific issues and by giving the necessary information to eliminate the states' uncertainty about each other's future preferences and behaviour.

Above all, the process of intergovernmental cooperation determines the attitude of individual states to the dynamics of integration, as well as the conditions according to which national governments will delegate their entitlements to supranational institutions. The cost of such a delegation, which goes beyond the monitoring functions of classical international regimes, is increased political risk. Functions of this type in the case of the EU include "competition policy" administered by the European Commission and the interpretation of the application of the EU law by the European Court of Justice (Moravcsik, 1993, p. 512).

Critics argue that the theory of liberal intergovernmentalism, as the theory of grand bargains, is incapable of explaining everyday decision-making, and thus is limited to only a small scope of the EU's policymaking in which institutions play a disproportionally small role. Moreover, Moravcsik and Schimmelfenning (2009) indicated that the theory is solely focused on conscious intergovernmental decision-making at the moment of amending the treaty, thus overlooking many unintended or undesired consequences that result from treaty amendments, simultaneously giving a rather misleading impression of the whole process of integration.

To sum up the considerations about modern political theories of integration, it is worth noting that both the fusion theory and the bargaining theory of international cooperation are relevant conceptual tools to assess the EU's policy coordination and have a potential to develop the theory of integration. The fusion theory explains different trajectories of the EU's integration process, by researching the interactions of various actors, contributing to the policymaking, to capture finally how they behave. It also shows the importance of growing interdependencies between supranational and national institutions, causing ultimately an increase of exchanges among different levels of governance as well as increased sharing of responsibilities. In turn, the bargaining theory of international cooperation draws attention to the significance of the issue of (different) national preferences and intergovernmental cooperation while researching the evolution of European integration.

1.2 Economic integration theories

In the light of the economic integration theories, economic integration is interpreted as a form of economic cooperation aimed at eliminating economic borders among states and creating a platform to unite national economics. Economic integration theories were researched and developed by, among others, Viner (1950), Tinbergen (1954), Scitovsky (1958), Balassa (1962, 1965) and Machlup (1977), and more contemporarily by Molle (2001), Pelkmans (2001) and Baldwin and Wyplosz (2009). In the theory of economic integration two stages of development can be distinguished, both address economic and political issues relevant for its time. The first stage includes the traditional theories of economic integration, which focus on the interpretation of possible benefits (and costs) of integration and are often referred to as a "static analysis". The second stage, commonly called a "dynamic analysis", embraces new economic integration theories, which were developed in different economic conditions and trade environment than the traditional theory. This part of the monography focuses on discussing traditional and new economic integration theories as well as the theories of economic integration for developing countries, including the training ground theory and the package approach.

1.2.1 Traditional economic integration theories

The theoretical studies on trade integration and preferential trade agreements are based on the seminal book by Viner (1950) entitled *The Customs Union Issue*, which is commonly recognised as the first research of the benefits of economic integration, critically analysed from a purely economic perspective. According to the author customs unions do not necessarily result in gains to members, although they do eliminate some tariffs. Viner (1950, p. 135) argued that "customs unions are not important and are unlikely to yield more economic benefit than harm, unless they are between sizable countries which practice substantial protection of substantially similar industries". To help understand this ambiguity, he presents a static analysis of economic integration, which distinguished the effects of trade creation and trade diversion. Viner perceived the first effect of customs unions as creating new trade flows between member states as a result of more effective allocation of resources and better labour division. In turn, the author understood trade diversion as replacing trade with more effective external suppliers with less efficient member states of the union. Viner (1950, p. 166) also claimed that "customs union is only a partial, uncertain, and otherwise imperfect mean of doing what a world-wide non-discriminatory reduction of trade barriers can do more fully, more certainly, and equitably". The author's theory practically means that countries will be highly motivated to integrate, if integration possibly brings more benefits than costs, i.e., when integration leads to more trade creation than trade diversion.

Viner's static analysis of economic integration effects was further researched and developed by Meade (1995, 1956), Lipsey (1957, 1960, 1970) and other scholars (Makower and Morton, 1953; Johnson, 1962; Kemp, 1969; Kemp and Wan, 1976; Chacholiades, 1978; Riezman, 1979, 1985, 1999; Kennan and Riezman, 1990; Lloyd, 1982; El-Agraa, 1983; Wooton, 1986; Robson, 1987), which allowed for distinguishing two additional effects of customs unions – the production effect and the consumption effect. In line with the production effect, higher-cost local products are replaced by cheaper imports from a partner country, whereas the consumption effect assumes that consumer demand of a given member state grows as local prices decrease to the price level of the customs union. An increase in both imports and consumer demand underlies the concept of trade creation. As a consequence of so understood trade creation, trade volumes grow and ultimately economic welfare increases. Hence, trade creation was recognised as a typically positive effect of the customs union, from the perspective of individual member states and the world economy. In turn, in trade diversion, the direction of supply is shifted from more- to less-efficient producers and the utilisation of production factors loses its efficiency. Hence, this process can be interpreted as a negative effect of the customs union.

While the production effect was taken into account by Viner, the consumption effect was not considered. The author's assumption that trade diversion is a negative phenomenon implies a welfare judgement, whereas this implication requires the combination of the two above-mentioned effects and not the only one. Although Viner's dichotomy of trade creation and trade diversion effects is fundamental to classify changes in the production effect, it cannot be applied to make assumptions concerning the economic welfare of customs unions (Lipsey, 1957; 1970; Gehrels, 1956; Krauss, 1972).

Subsequent studies on the issue of the production and consumption effects revealed that trade diversion may also be welfare-increasing, if welfare losses, resulting from the diversion to a higher-cost supplier country, are more than outweighed by welfare gains from the reduced process to consumers due to the elimination of tariff on imports, which results in an increased consumer surplus, irrespective of the fact whether the increased imports were from the least-cost supplier (Cooper and Massell, 1965, p. 742; Johnson, 1975, p. 117; Pomfret, 1997, p. 182). Viner's static analysis has been the driving force behind numerous research works that subsequently sought to address different issues of integration effects and to determine specific conditions under which customs unions would either improve or worsen economic welfare. All these studies concluded that no one-sided answer could be given to the issue of whether customs unions increase the economic welfare or not.

Lipsey (1960), in his further research, argued that the distinction between the production effect and the consumption effect of customs unions is not fully satisfactory. The author claimed that Viner's analysis emphasised substitution in production and undermined substitution in consumption. He pointed out that this classification is misleading because consumption changes will stimulate production changes, suggesting another distinction between inter-country substitution and inter-commodity substitution. The former is when one country is substituted by another in line with Viner's analysis of trade creation and trade diversion effects, whereas the latter occurs when one commodity is substituted by another as a result of the relative price change (Lipsey, 1960). The dissatisfaction with the trade creation–trade diversion classification was also reflected in the studies, among others, by Lipsey (1970), Kemp and Wan (1976), Riezman (1979), Lloyd (1982) and Wooton (1986), in which the authors, trying to develop other approaches to trade creation, introduced a new concept referred to as "the terms of trade-volume of trade approach", under which the impact on a regional trade agreement can be recognised by its effects on both – the terms of trade (prices) and the terms of trade volumes. This approach of terms of trade-volume utilises, instead of Viner's partial equilibrium, a general equilibrium analysis, which reflects the impact of the customs union on individual integrating countries, and not on the world's welfare

(Abrego, Riezman and Whalley, 2005). Additionally, previous studies investigating the welfare impact of economic integration assumed that the analysed country was a small country with no effect on world prices. However, Krauss (1972) claimed that it was not necessarily true. If a country is large enough to influence the world's prices, and if this country levies a tariff, then it will reduce the demand for imports. Consequently, the prices of these imported goods fall in world's markets relative to their exports, thus improving the terms of trade.

Concerning the terms of the trade volumes of international trade, the contributors to Viner's theory remarked that a customs union is more likely to produce welfare gains the higher the proportion of trade of the given country with its trading partner in the union is, and the lower the proportion with the rest of the world. Additionally, member states, which make a high proportion of their total expenditure on domestic trade, i.e., has a low volume of international trade as a percentage of their GDP, are more probable to benefit from economic integration (Lipsey, 1960; Spraos, 1964; Bhagwati, 1971).

Summing up, it can be concluded that in the traditional theory of economic integration, the trade creation–trade diversion effect is an important determinant allowing to estimate the gains of the customs union; nevertheless, the terms of trade-volume of trade approach constitute a noteworthy alternative to the traditional methodology.

1.2.2 New economic integration theories

Already in the 1960s it became obvious that the static analysis of trade creation and trade diversion is not sufficient and cannot fully assess the impact of integration on economic welfare. Therefore, Balassa (1962) introduced a new instrument to analyse the effects of economic integration on welfare – a dynamic effects analysis to better explain the reasons and economic rationale behind the establishment of customs unions and economic integration models. The dynamic effects of economic integration embrace a wide range of factors that may affect the economic growth rate of participating in the integration agreement member states: large-scale economies, technological change, the impact of integration on market structure and competition, productivity growth, risk and uncertainty as well as investment activity (Balassa, 1962; Cooper and Massell, 1965; Schiff and Winters, 1998).

In some studies, the concept of static effects and the development of the theory of economic integration, initiated by Viner and continued by his followers, are referred to as "old regionalism", whereas "new regionalism" is represented by the above-mentioned dynamic effects (Sheer, 1981; El-Agra, 1988; De Melo and Panagariya, 1993; Fernandez, 1997; Lawrence, 1997; Burfisher, Robinson and Thierfelder, 2003; UNCTAD, 2007). Other researchers distinguish between the "first regionalism", while referring to the static effects analysis and the "second regionalism" with regard to the dynamic effects analysis. There are also those, who differentiate the time framework within which the effects occur in the economy, i.e., "short-term static effects", which are related to the initial shift in the behaviour of economic actors and "long-term restructuring effects", which refer to the improvement of the condition for the functioning of companies, their efficiency and competition (Panusheff, 2003, p. 37).

The dynamic analysis of the effects of economic integration is based on the features of the contemporary free economy. Therefore, with regard to their deeper scope, dynamic effects have a more significant impact on the proceeding economic processes in comparison to static effects. As Marinov (2014, p. 167) argued the only obvious drawback of the dynamic analysis of the effects of economic integration, in contrast to the static analysis, is the fact there is practically no fully reliable method for quantitative assessment of these dynamic effects.

To conclude, in the light of the new theories of economic integration, the impetus behind previous integration efforts (trade creation and trade diversion) was entirely different from that which has triggered the recent integration processes, embracing, among others, the participation of private sector, foreign direct investment and an increasing role of services. Together with these driving forces, the causes and effects of the dynamic analyses of economic integration also include, e.g., economies of scale, economies of scope, investment creation and investment diversion, consolidation of production and increase of its specialisation, improvement of the organisation and management of production and production technology, rationalisation of territorial distribution and utilisation of resources, increase of production efficiency and increase in competition (Corden, 1972; Balassa and Stoutjesdijk, 1975; Baldwin, Forslid and Haaland, 1995; Lawrence, 1997; Marinov, 1999; Panusheff, 2003).

1.3 Theories of economic integration for developing countries

In most cases, the theories of economic integration and its effects – both the dynamic and the static ones – are believed not to be fully applicable to integration agreements among developing and least developed countries. Already, Balassa (1965) claimed that the theoretical literature of economic integration preliminarily addresses the issue of the customs union among industrialised countries, whose problems are not that much related to economic development, but more to adjustments in production and consumption arrangements. Consequently, many studies rejected the traditional theory of the customs union, arguing that Viner's analysis of economic integration has limited relevance or even is irrelevant for developing countries (Meier, 1960; Abdel Jaber, 1971; Andic, Andic and Dosser, 1971). As a result, new theories of economic integration appeared in the literature, which were adjusted to the special characteristics and needs of developing countries (see e.g., Allen, 1961; Bhambri, 1962; Mikesell, 1965; Kahnert et al., 1969; Andic, Andic and Dosser, 1971).

The traditional theory of economic integration concerns numerous factors and effects of economic integration to conclude that the net static effect determines the welfare effect, which influences the countries' motivation to participate in the integration process. In the case of developing countries, these factors and effects of economic integration can be divided into three main groups: (1) general economic effects; (2) market-related effects and (3) trade-related effects (Marinov, 2014).

The general economic factors and effects of integration agreements can be analysed from the perspective of economic development, macroeconomic coordination policy and the (economic) size of participating countries. Abdel Jaber (1971) and Balassa and Stoutjesdij (1975) argued that for developing countries, economic integration should be treated as an instrument for their economic development,[6] including poverty reduction, support for the facilitation of healthcare and education systems as well as regional security, and not that much as customs and/or trade policies. In turn, Kahnert et al. (1969) and Hirshman (1971) argued that, for the durability of trade agreements, it is necessary for integrating countries to unify their internal monetary and foreign exchange policies, which could be even more important in promoting the reciprocal trade exchange than the customs preferences themselves. In line with the traditional integration theory, the benefits of integration are directly proportional to the size (in economic terms) of participating countries. Balassa (1962) added that integration gains also depend on the countries' rate of economic growth. Therefore, as developing economies tend to grow at higher rates than the already developed ones, the benefits of integration for them would be even bigger. Kreinin (1964) argued that potential gains from economic integration can be more visible for small and medium sized member states, particularly if integration proceeds between a small (developing) country and a large (developed) country because there is more demand for its exports. However, the opponents to this approach maintained that the disproportions of gains in favour of the larger economy are inevitable, and the small country is an unequal partner, forced to adjust to the economic and price structure relevant for the larger member state.

As far as the market-related factors and effects of economic integration are concerned, it is worth noting that welfare effects for developing countries should not only be limited to the consumption and production side, but they should also have a positive impact on employment, productivity, product specialisation and international competitiveness. Regarding the first two factors – employment and productivity – it can be stated that the majority of developing countries are characterised by relatively low productivity, together with mounting unemployment. However, the trade diversion effect of economic integration may increase their welfare, causing the labour force to be transferred from low-productive sectors to the ones with higher value-added. Longi and Nijkamp (2007) pointed to the fact that integration benefits to employment are also related to changes in the geographical distribution of production, which influence labour demand; bigger flows of workers contribute to greater labour force supply, which, in turn, increases employment opportunities.

When it comes to product specialisation, it can be argued that most developing countries are characterised by specialising in the production of primary goods, and the economic surplus gained from this type of production is rarely relocated and efficiently invested in other sectors. Hence, to accelerate economic growth, they usually advocate a policy of diversification and import substitution. However, as Demas (1965) remarked, they can also achieve balanced economic growth through economic integration by increasing the size of the market, benefiting from the economies of scale and expanding their inter-industry transitions.

Economic integration can also be perceived by developing economies as an instrument for greater competitiveness in world economy. This approach aims at making economic integration policies of developing countries compatible with and complementary to other policies to promote international competitiveness. Already Viner (1950) argued that countries manufacturing competing (similar) products gain more benefits from integration than those producing the complementary (different) ones. This assumption should put developing countries in a favourable position since they preliminary specialise in exporting products of the primary sector, thus, in Viner's sense, the competing ones. However, as Balassa (1965) and Abdel Jaber (1971) argued, a major part of their exports is usually directed to developed economies, which, in fact, reduces the gains from economic integration because it does not increase the volume of intra-regional trade. Hence, they should strive for achieving a significant degree of complementarity, simultaneously increasing the volume of their intra-regional trade. Subsequent studies continued to support the assumption that in the case of developing countries integration among the complementary (heterogeneous) economies is more beneficial for them than among the competing (homogenous) ones (Inotai, 1999).

As far as the trade-related group of factors and effects of economic integration is concerned a number of studies proved that trade diversion may be beneficial for developing countries for several reasons (Demas, 1965; Sakamoto, 1969). First, integration increases the size of the market and enables the reduction of costs through the economies of scale. Second, import substitution over a wider area will allow the integrated region as a whole to spend more foreign currency for the import of capital goods, thus contributing to an increase in investment and eventually to economic growth. Furthermore, owing to trade diversification consumers can purchase imported goods at lower prices after the removal of tariffs, thus increasing consumer surplus. However, as Elkan (1975) noted, these effects should be weighed against losses in tariff revenues in this process, on which most of the developing countries rely, as the main source of the whole government revenues.[7]

Another important trade-related aspect of integration among developing countries regards the initial tariff levels. Meade (1956) assumed that the higher initial rates of tariffs between integrating countries are the higher the expected gains of integration will be. In the case of most developing countries, national tariffs are rather high, mainly because of their striving to increase revenues or to protect national industry. It is worth mentioning here that already Viner (1950) claimed that in some circumstances, economic integration can be a move towards free trade, but in other cases it is as a step towards more protection, and protection trade regimes can turn beneficial for developing countries. For example, assuming that one of the main aims of economic integration of developing countries is to support their industrial development, it could be achieved through protection since integration is regarded as equal to import substitution, which, in turn, is an instrument to promote national industry.

It is also worth considering the relation between international trade as a share of GDP and potential benefits from economic integration. Lipsey (1957) assumed that the lower share of international trade in GDP of integrating countries is the greater expected gains from integration on welfare will be. This becomes a matter of great importance for developing countries because international trade as a percentage of GDP in low-income countries is usually lower than in countries with high level of income (although this imbalance has decreased recently). However, it should be emphasised that this assumption does not apply to economies with medium levels of income or the least developed countries, for which the share of trade in GDP is even more important than that in the high-income ones.

There is a widespread view that one of the best indicators of the success of economic integration is the increase in the share of intra-regional trade in total trade of member states. However, it should be stressed here that the growth of intra-regional trade may result from trade diversion from more efficient and competitive non-member states. Thus, it can be recognised as a positive effect of economic integration, provided that it is related to improving the world's competitiveness as a whole.

Trade-related effects of economic integration among developing countries are also connected to the change of trade structure with developed economies. It is widely recognised that a major part of imports from developed countries to the developing ones consists of capital goods. From the perspective of the dynamic analysis, economic integration of developing countries requires substantial investment. Due to the fact that most of it is imported from developed economies in the form of capital goods, the volume of imports of integrating developing countries is likely to grow. Hence, it can be concluded that the long-term aim of economic integration among developing countries should not be the reduction of trade with third countries, but rather a change in their trade structure (Mikesell, 1965). However, if economic integration among developing countries results in the trade diversion of consumer goods, then it will release more foreign currency for imports of capital goods from developed countries outside the integration agreement. The volume of trade with third countries may not change or it may even increase, but what matters is the fact that it changes its structure (Sakamoto, 1969, p. 293).

While considering the trade-related effects of integration among developing countries, transport infrastructure should also be taken into account. Transport costs reduce the potential benefits of trade integration for member states; hence, distance has an impact on inter-sectorial trade. This is particularly important for developing countries – being comparable in terms of GDP per capita, they are more dependent on intra-sectorial trade, and transport infrastructure is rather in a poor condition there. Balassa (1965) remarked that transport costs between two neighbouring developing countries may be even higher than those between them and a further located developed country.

It is argued that to assess integration processes among developing countries, more attention should be paid to dynamic rather than static effects while assessing integration processes among developing countries. Rueda-Junquera (2006) emphasised that the traditional economic integration theory, analysing the static effects of resource allocation, implies relatively small gains for developing countries; therefore, they should seek the motivation for concluding integration agreements preliminary in the dynamic analysis of integration and the effects it entails. Moreover, the traditional economic integration theory is heavily based on the neoclassical assumptions of full employment, perfect competition, constant returns of scale and perfect mobility of production factors, thus confining to the study of the static effects of economic integration, whereas dynamic effects of economic integration may lead to higher rates of economic growth and greater exploitation of unused economic potential.

In considerations on the causes and effects of integration agreements for developing countries, except for the static and dynamic analyses, more complex theories should be mentioned – the training ground theory and the package approach. The aforementioned issues, such as international competitiveness, production specialisation and industrial protection for the sake of stimulating industrial development in economic integration schemes of developing countries, are more thoroughly discussed in the training ground theory. This theory is based on the assumption that during the first phase of integration among developing countries, their international competitiveness can be gradually improved by relying on the regional market in the initial phase of industrialisation. Free trade among member states together with the frequently high common external tariff on imports from third countries should ensure temporary protection of infant industries and a sufficiently large market for future industrial development. This process referred to as "import-substituting industrialisation" will secure sufficient time for the development of the industrial sectors of developing member states (Rueda-Junquera, 2006, p. 4).

The openness to world markets may proceed at a later stage when developing countries reach an appropriate level of efficiency and technical development. Therefore, economic integration among developing countries may be recognised as a transitional period towards an open economy and competition with third countries after a short period of training. One of the arguments against this theory is the fact that developing regional markets are often not large enough to enable the industrial development or provide the economy of scale advantages. Furthermore, as a result of the training process, a relatively small (or even no at all) improvement takes place. Additionally, there are visible differences in demand preferences and tastes regarding imports from the rest of non-member states compared to those participating in intra-regional trade. Last but not least, protection may actually become permanent instead of being only temporary (Inotai, 1999).

In turn, the package approach, which is another complex way to pursue integration among developing countries, strives at facilitating the integration process and increasing the stability of an integration agreement, by ensuring that each member state is in charge of implementing a single integration project within a common package of projects. The elements covered by such a package of projects may include, e.g., transport, communication, public goods, education, science, agriculture and mining industry (Balassa and Stoutjesdijk, 1975).

To conclude, on the basis of the conducted analysis it can be stated that the majority of scholars express doubts concerning the applicability of the static approach to the causes and effects of economic integration among developing countries. Instead, they share the opinion that the dynamic approach, which aims at achieving long-term economic growth in integrating economies, should be the appropriate justification for economic integration among developing countries. It is also worth noting that whereas in the case of developed economies, the main rationale for economic integration preliminarily comes from economic groups of stakeholders, in developing countries, integration processes are often initiated for political reasons, which may sometimes lead to unsatisfactory economic outcomes.

Notes

1 This approach refers to the Wiener's (1950) cybernetic model, who applied the index of transactions among people. The higher index, the better-established relations among the participants of a process. In turn, such developed interactions and mass communication lead to the creation of the community of security.

2 In the modern period, the Constitution of the USA of 1787 is recognised as the first experiment in establishing a federal system of government. Next, federalism as a mode of political organisation was embodied in the Constitutions of Swiss Confederation (1848) and the Dominion of Canada (1867) and the Commonwealth of Australia (1900); see Rath (1978).

3 The international relations (IR) theory distinguishes between rationalism and social constructivism – the dichotomy transposed into the integration theory by Pollack (2001). Rationalism comprises such theories as realism, liberal intergovernmentalism, institutionalism of rational choice and principal-agent theory, whereas social constructivism embraces neofunctionalism, sociological institutionalism, theory of organisation and gender theory.

4 The main idea behind the federalism theory is the assumption of the existence of an unavoidable conflict in the society (Burges, 1998). Hence, the appeal of the federal idea to many Europeans preliminary resulted from both the threat of war and practical experience of World War II.

5 In this period, the cooperation on coal and steel under the ECSC "spilled over" into EEC and EAEC (Euratom). Additionally, the schedule of the formation of the customs union and the progress made on the Common Agricultural Policy supported the neofunctionalist assumptions.

6 Whereas economic integration is more focused on better resource allocation, the development theory preliminary concerns benefits resulting from rapid, long-term economic growth and from the utilisation of under-employed (or not employed at all) resources and production factors.

7 In the literature the term of "efficient trade diversion" can be found. It means that if economic integration among developing countries leads to trade diversion, it should not reduce welfare since the production substitution will occur from an efficient developed non-member country towards the relatively efficient developing member country of the integration agreement, thus creating benefits in terms of employment and income within the community (Sakamoto, 1969).

2 Economic integration, institutions and institutionalisation – terminological and conceptual systematisation

Before conducting the study on the character, evolution and outcomes of East Asia's economic integration, the author makes an attempt to systemise the knowledge about economic integration and institutionalisation processes. To realise this aim, the term of economic integration as well as related terms of regional economic integration, regionalism and regionalisation are discussed to proceed subsequently to the interpretation of the notions of an institution and institutionalisation, embedding the analyses in the theory of new institutional economics (NIE). The considerations of this chapter are complemented with the presentation of different institutional forms and models of economic integration.

2.1 Economic integration, regionalism and regionalisation

The term "integration" has an interdisciplinary character. It is used in many scientific fields; thus, it is differently and multidimensionally interpreted. Referring to the etymology of the term, the verb "integrate", from Latin *integratus*, means "to render (something) whole, bring together the parts of" (Online Etymology Dictionary, 2024). Going back to the roots of the term, "integration" appeared for the first time in the early 1930s in two separate publications – in a book written by two German authors, Gaedicke and Eynern (1933), on trade statistics and in an English translation of the Swedish edition of Heckscher's (1935) work on mercantilism. It is believed that, in the late 1930s and early 1940s, the latter attracted a wide group of readers, among others, Röpke, Mises, Bonn, Hayek and Hilgerdt, who applied the term "integration/disintegration" referring to international trade.

The term "integration" was adopted for the official use a decade later than it appeared for the first time in the publications by the above-mentioned authors. It was yet not used either in Churchill's speech delivered at the University of Zurich in 1946, when he called for the "recreation of the European family",[1] or in the "Marshall Plan" speech at Harvard University in 1947.[2] However,

DOI: 10.4324/9781003544234-2

as Machlup (1977) assumed, the Marshall's speech might have included the term as, among the draft documents, there was found a paper written by three authors – Clevelan, Moore and Kindleberger, in which they called for "a coordinated European Recovery Plan" directed "toward a strong and economically integrated Europe". Since then, the term was applied in an increasing number of speeches and documents. For example, the term "economic integration" was used by the Administrator of the Economic Cooperation Administration, Hoffmann, in his official pronouncement to the Council of the Organisation of European Economic Cooperation in October 1949, while elaborating on important tasks for a further progress towards the integration of the Western European economy. He maintained that

> the first major task – that of balancing Europe's trade with the dollar area – its performance will not be meaningful unless we have come to grips with our second task – the building of an expanding economy in Western Europe through economic integration.[3]

Whereas in the 1950s, the term "integration" was still vaguely defined, as Price (1955, p. 122) remarked, the world reflected "an adaptation to diverse currents of thought on both sides of the Atlantic (…) though never precisely defined, connoted more than casual cooperation but less than full unification", currently an abundance of its definitions can be found in the literature. With reference to the economy, scholarship distinguished three main approaches to integration: (1) economic liberalistic approach; (2) idealistic approach and (3) dirigiste approach.

Economic liberalists, e.g., Allais (1958, 1960), Röpke (1957, 1959) and Heilperin (1957), associated economic integration with the liberalisation of trade and payments within a specific group of states. Following this approach, it means the abolition of barriers to commodity markets. For example, Allais (1958, p. 65) argued that "practically, the only mutually acceptable rule for close economic cooperation between democratic societies is the rule of the free market". Allais (1960) further emphasised that economic integration can take place only on the basis of the market mechanism, whose credo is competition. Trade liberalisation and the creation of a common market (CM) aim at maximalising social benefits within the integrating group of states. It can be achieved in terms of perfect competition with the implementation of four principles: (1) the principle of identical prices; (2) the principle of consumer freedom; (3) the principle of seller's orders and (4) the profitability principle. Integrating states should strive for abolishing all trade barriers while simultaneously implementing the aforementioned principles. The liberalisation of the market economy leads to free movement of goods, capital and workers, which, according to Allais (1960), constitutes the nature of the concept of integration.

In turn, Röpke (1959) perceived economic integration as a state of affairs, which enables to conduct trade relations equally freely and equally effectively, like those that exist inside the national economy. The author also argued that European economic integration is nothing else than an attempt to cure the disintegration of the post-1914 that damaged the previous integration of national economies (Röpke, 1957).

To a certain extent, a similar stance to economic liberalists in this matter was represented by Balassa (1962), who defined economic integration as a process and as a state of affairs. The author argued that "regarded as a process, it encompasses measures designed to abolish discrimination between economic units belonging to different national states; viewed as a state of affairs, it can be represented by the absence of various forms of discrimination between national economies" (Balassa, 1962, p. 1). It is worth, here, stressing that economic integration can be perceived in a static or dynamic manner, i.e., as a process or as a state of affairs reached by this process. For example, Marjolin (1955) represented a dynamic approach to economic integration, defining it as each process, which leads to a greater degree of unity. Similar to Balassa (1961), Kahnert et al. (1975) perceived economic integration as the process of progressively removing discriminations that occur at national borders. In turn, Machlup (1977) viewed economic integration as a process of combining separate economies into larger economic regions.

According to the idealistic approach, economic integration is perceived as a certain ideal of international relations or as a social–systemic concept. The proponents of this approach believed that integration should aim at creating a greater equality all over the world and greater participation of individual states in the contemporary civilisation; hence, it should embrace not only economic but also political and social factors. For example, Myrdal (1956) emphasised the equality of opportunity in the integrated economy, also adding that the remuneration paid for productive services must be equal, regardless of racial, social and cultural differences.

In turn, Kindleberger (1963), referring to Tinbergen (1954), Balassa (1962) and Myrdal's (1956) concept of integration, established the definition of economic integration based on three components: (1) free trade; (2) the absence of all forms of discrimination (presumably going beyond the free trade into wage, tax and other aspects of economic policy, which might impinge on trade) and (3) factor price equalisation. According to Kindleberger (1963), the equality of factor prices – which is relatively rarely achieved between trading partners, since regarded as non-operational – helps, in fact, to determine connections among economic, social and political integration.

Scholars, representing the idealistic approach, also believed that economic integration should strive for achieving the optimal economic policy. For example, Tinbergen (1954, p. 95) claimed that

> integration may be said to be the creation of the most desirable structure of international economy, removing artificial hindrances to the optimal

> operation and introducing deliberately all desirable elements of coordination or unification. The problem of integration therefore forms part of a more general problem namely that of the optimum economic policy.

An extreme approach to the liberalist solution is the dirigiste approach to economic integration, according to which “integration could also be achieved through state trading and through the coordination of national economic plans without the lifting of trade barriers. This alternative rejects the use of market methods and relies solely on administrative, nonmarket means” (Balassa, 1962, p. 8). Such a pattern of integration was found, for example, in the integration projects of Soviet-type economies. The functioning of the Council of Mutual Economic Assistance, comprising the Soviet Union and its European satellite countries, was based on the coordination of long-term plans and bilateral trade agreements. The need for centralised economic planning in a union was advocated by, e.g., Philip (1957, p. 225), who argued that “there is no alternative to a directed economy” because “the market can be extended not by liberalising but by organising”. Although this tendency did not mean a return to the pre-1914 situation, it caused an increased use of the market mechanism and contributed to a substantial economic growth of the European countries during the 1950s (Balassa, 1962).

Whereas scholars seem to share the common opinion that integration can be interpreted as a process or/and as a state of affairs, it is not always obvious what is to be integrated – people, areas, markets, production, goods, resources, etc. – and what are the fundamental criteria of such integration? There is a group of proponents of the approach that integration preliminary means the integration of the economic policy or politics in general. Moreover, in the case of European integration, economic integration is only a means to political integration. For example, Sannwald and Stohler (1969) argued that political considerations are even more important than the economic ones, especially in Europe, where integration is more a political rather than economic issue. Hallstein (1962) claimed that the emergence of new, large superpowers is a constant encouragement for older, smaller states to search for measures to ensure their influences by replacing the former rivalry between them with effective, common cooperation. Hence, this is not the economy that is integrated, but the politics.

To conclude, in the literature, there is no homogenous, commonly used definition of economic integration. Nevertheless, it seems that a common consensus can be achieved with regard to, at least, three issues. First, economic integration refers, in principle, to the division of labour. Second, it involves the mobility of goods, services and/or production factors (capital and labour). Third, it is connected to the issue of discrimination or non-discrimination in the treatment of goods, services and/or production factors (e.g., with respect to their origin or destination) at national borders.

Economic integration is inherently associated with the term of a region. Thus, in the literature, the terms of regional economic integration as well as regionalism and regionalisation are also distinguished. The criterion for this distinction is preliminarily determined by the number of countries participating in integration processes – regional integration allows for the participation of all (or the majority of) countries of a specific region. Misala (2005) defines regional economic integration as the process of reducing the degree of the separation of commodity markets and production factors from each other as well as mitigating all types of problems within the specified groupings.

Regional economic integration can be perused along three processes, which may overlap; hence, Pascha (2004) and Soesastro (2006) distinguished between: (1) market-driven integration (happens more or less spontaneously); (2) functional integration (embraces the efforts of liberalisation and the facilitation of cooperation in a coordinated or concerted manner with the aim to promote further market integration) and (3) institutional integration (involves the establishment of a mechanism/organisation that will move and deepen the process of regional integration). When governments embark on regional cooperation and agree to implement collective action plans and programmes, they are promoting functional cooperation that could lead to functional integration.

In deliberations on regional economic integration, the terms of regionalism and regionalisation should also be discussed. In early studies on regionalism, Nye (1968) interpreted it as the creation of international associations or groupings on the basis of a region, perceived preliminary through the prism of geographical conditions. Moreover, these associations of states are not only connected to each other by close geographical proximity, but also by specific interdependencies. Similarly, Haliżak (1999) defined regionalism as all possible forms of international cooperation, like different alliances and associations of integrating countries, which are geographically located close to each other. The foundation of such a cooperation among countries is their common interests resulting not only from immediate neighbourhood, but also similar social and political systems, comparable level of economic development and economic complementarity as well as common cultural elements, including language, tradition, history, religion and attitude toward the state. Carpenter (2008), in turn, did not limit the process of regionalism to countries that are of close geographical proximity, but also expands it to include countries located in different parts of the globe.

Regionalism can evolve and in this evolving process at least four stages can be distinguished (Haliżak, 1999):

- emergence of regional awareness among elites and social classes in neighbouring countries. The pace and range of shaping such awareness depends on the degree of the ethnic, racial, language, religious and cultural homogeneity of people inhabiting the given region as well as the sense of common historical destiny and common experience of past cooperation,
- revealing the common needs and interests of societies inhabiting the specific region (e.g., the activities of European federalists proclaiming the

slogan of the union of nations after World War II, represented by Spinelli, Monnet, Schuman, Churchill and Adenauer),

- a quantitative and qualitative increase of positive relations among states and societies of the region, leading to their regulation at the institutional level, e.g., in a form of the system of regional consultations and conferences as well as norms of regional law,
- integration of states in the region, as the most advanced stage of the development of regionalism, leading to an increase of the entitlements of supranational institutions at the expense of member states in terms of decision-making competences.

The processes in the above-mentioned stages of the development of regionalism lead to the selection of regional systems, which do not adequately cover the meaning of the term of geographical region since, contemporarily, other criteria than the geographical ones seem to be more important. Therefore, in the literature, the term of regionalisation is often used, which Haliżak (1999) understood as the activity of selecting regions on the basis of defined criteria and research methods or the regional policy of member countries in a given grouping. Regionalisation understood as the practical activity associated with the regional policy is reflected by eliminating barriers impeding the communication of communities within the region, creating new regional principles and legal norms, concluding regional agreements to ensure peace, security and peaceful settlement of disputes as well as establishing regional organisations. The most advanced form of regional policy is the establishment of a supranational organisational structure, gaining the competences of national governments.

In turn, Haggard (1993) defined regionalisation as an economic process, in which trade and investment in a particular region grow more rapidly than outside the region. A similar approach is also represented by Camilleri (2003), who associated regionalisation with economic flows and processes, but additionally enlarged it by technological and social-cultural factors, which tie member states with each other in the region.

Regionalism and regionalisation were also thoroughly reviewed by Mansfield and Solingen (2010), who pointed out to difficulties in conceptualising the researched notions. The authors argue that regionalism usually refers to the political dimension as well as cooperation and coordination of states located in geographical closeness to each other, whereas regionalisation is related to the economic process, within which the economic flows of trade and investment grow more rapidly within the group of countries belonging to the same geographical region than between these countries and the rest of the world.

In considerations on regional economic integration, especially with regard to East Asian countries, it is also worth mentioning the term "open regionalism", which is embedded in and originates from economic cooperation efforts in the Asia-Pacific. Definitions differentiate "open" regionalism from the "closed" regionalism. The usual criterion for such distinction is a clear shift from an inward-looking, import substituting focus, which prevailed in the regional integration movement of earlier decades, to a greater emphasis on outward-oriented and internationally competitive strategies (Kuwayama, 1999). Also, open regionalism is sometimes interchangeably used to refer to "new" regionalism, whose main features are the liberalisation not only of goods but also of services and production factors, the harmonisation of regulatory regimes and the emergence of North-South regional agreements. The term "new" also underlines inclusivity of membership, as opposed to a regionalism based on exclusivity (Hallett and Primo Braga, 1994; Mistry, 1995). An important criterion is open membership in the regional arrangement – any country willing to accept the rules of the regional arrangement could be admitted. Another version of new, open regionalism refers to the multidimensional process of regional integration that includes economic, political, social and cultural aspects (Hettne and Inotai, 1994).

Considering the researched subject matter of this monography and the direction of analyses, it is also necessary to introduce the term "institutionalised regionalism", which will be used here interchangeably with the term "institutionalised economic integration". Here, institutionalised regionalism combines the characteristics of institution-driven, regional and economic integration and is defined as the separation of an economic organism from the world economy as a result of policy decisions taken by the governments of the countries belonging to the same region in order to promote economic cooperation under the terms of a free trade agreement (FTA).

2.2 Institutions, institutionalisation and new institutional economics

The term "institutionalisation" originates from Latin *institutio*, meaning "a disposition, arrangement; instruction, education" (Online Etymology Dictionary, 2024). In the contemporary literature, an explicit distinction between an "institution" and "institutionalisation" has been introduced. Both terms are closely intertwined; however, the initial term is "institution". Already Aristoteles, Cicero and Confucius argued that institutions constituted the foundation for each civilisation. Over the centuries, the role of institutions in the social life has been increasing, which led to coining the term "institutionalisation" at the end of the 19th century. The term "institution" can be used in at least two meanings, such as:

- an established organisation or corporation (e.g., school, bank, office), especially of a public character, which deals with a specific range of issues and runs a certain activity, especially the non-productive one. The term "institution" in the meaning "establishment or organization for the promotion of some charity" is used from the1700s.

- the creation of the set of legal or social norms, which constitute the basis for organising a certain area of life. The meaning of an institution as "established law or practice" was adopted into official use in the 1550s.

In the literature, scholars perceive institutions in a different way (Williamson, 1985, 1994; Keohane, 1989; North, 1990; Hodgson, 1996; Nee, 1998; Peters, 1999; Thelen, 1999; Campell, 2004; Greif, 2006; Scott, 2008, 2010). For example, Williamson (1985) perceived institutions through the prism of four levels. The first level, which constitutes the institutional foundation, is composed of informal institutions, such as customs, tradition, religious and cultural norms. The second level is created by formal institutions, such as constitutional principles, justice, ownership right, contract law as well as the system of administration, i.e., institutions restricting the possibilities of economic fraud. At the third level, there are non-governmental organisations, foundations and trade unions, i.e., the institutional surroundings, in which the principles of exchange, competition and the alternative use of resources are specified as well as new institutional solutions are elaborated, which, in turn, constitute the fourth level. Hence, at the last level there are institutions of the real economic life – market institutions. According to North (1990, p. 3), institutions are "the humanly devised constraints that shape human action"; they are constrained by both formal and informal conditions (e.g., law, property rights, culture, customs and tradition). The author also introduced the distinction between formal and informal institutions, arguing that the former ones are characterised by definite organisational structures, whereas the latter are perceived through the prism of the norms of behaviour, the principles of actions or the systems of values typical of a given society.

Likewise, Keohane (1989) associated institutions with a set of durable and interconnected formal and informal rules, determining the roles of subjects, shaping their expectations and restricting their behaviours. North (1990) observed that the effectiveness of informal rules can be enhanced by formal rules, embracing political and judicial rules, economic rules and contracts. As Mahoney and Thelen (2012) argued formal rules may also be enacted to verify, alter or replace informal constraints.

Scott (2008, p. 48) perceived institutions from a sociological perspective, defining them as "social structures that have attained a high degree of resilience [and are] composed of cultural-cognitive, normative, and regulative elements that, together with associated activities and resources, provide stability and meaning to social life". According to the author, this three-pillar framework of regulative, normative and cultural-cognitive elements emphasises the role of symbolic processes in social life, but in a broader sense, unless these symbolic systems provide guidelines for human activities and social relations, and unless they are related to human and physical resources, they are "emasculated". In other words, "to be of interest of social analysts, social institutions must be 'inhabited' by human actors" (Scott, 2010, p. 7).

In turn, the term "institutionalisation", a derivate of "institution", is applied to determine similar phenomena as those described as institutions, whereas the difference between them is that "institutionalisation" is associated with a certain dynamism of the process, which constitutes the basis for institutions. According to the "Great Dictionary of Foreign Words", the term can have, at least, two meanings:

- adding the character of an institution to certain actions and activities. This can refer to different actions and levels on which particular activities are undertaken (local, central, regional, sub-regional, global). According to the criterion of openness, institutions may admit all those, who are willing to participate in them, or only those, who fulfil certain conditions. Actions undertaken by institutions can be obligatory or voluntary, as well as specialised (e.g., financial, health, truism, development of security issues). Also, institutions of wider competences can be distinguished, e.g., the European Union (EU) or the United Nations.
- a "process of consolidating norms and patterns of behaviour recognised by the society as well as achieving the organisational and substantive bases by it".

According to Selznick (1957) institutionalisation is a process that emphasises stability and durability. The author argued that it is

> something that happens to an organisation over time, reflecting the organisation's own distinctive history, the people who have been in it, the groups it embodies and the vested interests they have created, and the way it has adapted to its environment.
>
> (Selznick, 1957, pp. 16–17)

In turn, Ruggie (1998) associated institutionalisation with coordinating and setting the patterns of behaviours; they should be stimulated in one rather than many directions, which are theoretically and empirically possible.

It is worth mentioning here that the process of institutionalisation has evolved over the centuries, and in its development several stages can be distinguished. Initially, it included solutions applied locally by tribes, then it was developed in the act of creating states. The next stage in its evolution was introducing principles that determined the system of international law with regard to international trade and maritime transport, as well as creating coalitions within organised communities and on global scale. Subsequently, institutionalisation reached its most advanced form, connected to evolutionary changes occurring in world economy, and amongst other, to the establishment of an extensive network of norms and legal institutions, in which membership is desired by states worldwide. The contemporary phase in the evolution of institutionalisation, created in the second half of the 20th century, can be supplemented by communities, ensuring regional economic security as well as integrating regional economies (Keohane, 1989).

Institutionalisation may lead to the creation of durable and purposefully cooperating sets of actions at the international level, which are the driving force of multilateral cooperation in the world economy. The perfect form of such a cooperation is the international institutions. Although their establishment began in the 19th century, and their revival was dated after the World War II, the idea of institutionalising the cooperation among the subjects of international law has accompanied people since ancient times. The first attempts of cooperation were manifested already in ancient Greece in a form of so called *amphictyonies* (places of religious worship) and *symmachies* (military alliances). Another embryonic form of an international institution present throughout the recorded history was the late medieval Hanseatic League as well as the Swiss Confederacy and the United Provinces of the Netherlands in modern history. However, it was not until the 19th century that international institutions in their present forms were first established, which was justified by the fact that the international system of states (at least in Europe) was not stable enough to allow for seeking different forms of cooperation (Archer, 1992). Initially, cooperation among countries began in the area of transport and communication. As the forerunner of the modern international institution, the Rhine Commission can be recognised, which was created in the 1980s to deal, on regular basis, with the issues of navigation and pollution on the Rhine. Subsequently, it was followed by the establishment of other river commissions; also, other modes of transport and communication emerged, e.g., the International Telegraphic Union, followed by the Universal Postal Union. Other areas did not lag behind; in the field of economics, the Metric Union, the International Copyright Union and the International Sugar Union were established. The breakthrough in the creation of international institutions was the Versailles Peace Settlement, which followed the World War I. Woodrow Wilson in his "fourteen points" speech called for creating "a general association of nations … under specific covenants for the purpose of affording mutual quarantines of political independence and territorial integrity to great and small states like".[4] The US president's plea contributed to the formation of the League of Nations, which was the first international institution, which was designed not just to organise cooperation between states in the areas of so called "low politics", like e.g., transport and communication, health or economics, but with its specific aims to guarantee peace and the establishment of the collective security system (Klabbers, 2009). Although the League of Nations failed in its own purpose – preventing war – it paved the way for the future development of international institutions. Already during the World War II, the urge to organise came back with a new impetus. In 1941, Roosevelt and Churchill concluded the Atlantic Charter, which served as the basis for the Declaration of the wartime allies and later for the Charter of the United Nations (Gardner, 1970). Also in 1944, the future of economic cooperation was mapped in Bretton Woods, where there was concluded an agreement on the need for the cooperation on the monetary and trade issues, leading finally to the establishment of, amongst other, the International Monetary Fund and the General Agreement on Tariffs and Trade. After the World War II, Europe also faced the rise of numerous international institutions. The Council of Europe was established, which was born out of Churchill's desire to create the United States of Europe, so that Europe would become an important power alongside the USA.[5] Additionally, to manage the American Marshall aid, the Organisation for European Economic Cooperation and Development was created, which was later transformed into the Organisation for Economic Co-operation and Development. Over time, international institutions started to emerge all over the world.

Except for specialised international institutions, emphasising the supremacy of the common social interest over the interests of particular countries, in the 1950s, in Europe, one more form of the institutionalisation of multilateral cooperation emerged – namely supranational institutions, i.e., European Coal and Steel Community, European Economic Community and European Community for Atomic Energy (Euratom). As Roche (1999) argued their functioning reflected not only the limitation of the role of the state in international relations to the advantage of multilateral structures, but also introduced a new type of relation between the civil society and public authorities.

Currently, there is observed an increased interest in institutions and institutionalisation in theoretical and empirical studies of different scientific disciplines (e.g., economics, law, sociology, political science). In the field of economics, it can largely be attributed to the development of NIE, which aims to "explain what institutions are, how they arise, what purposes they serve, how they change and how - if at all - they should be reformed" (Klein, 2000, p. 456). The term was coined by Williamson (1975), who wanted to highlight the differences between the new economic ideas and the "old" institutional economics. NIE traced its origins to Coase's (1937) analysis of the firm, Hayek's (1937, 1939, 1945) works on economics and knowledge and Chandler's (1962) history of industrial enterprise, along with the contributions by, among others, Simon (1961), Davis and North (1971), Alchian and Demsetz (1972) and Williamson (1975, 1985). There are many essential differences between the "new" and the "old" institutionalism. The analysis of the "old" institutional economics is mostly based on formal institutions and the role of society in defining values, whereas the NIE's approach is more individualistic; it originates from individual behaviour through interactions among individuals (Parada, 2005). According to North (1990, p. 3), institutions are "the humanly devised constraints that shape human action"; they are constrained by both formal and informal conditions (e.g., law, property rights, culture, customs and tradition). Another difference regards the role of rationality. According to the "older" approach to institutionalism, habits, norms and institutions play a significant role in directing human behaviour without rejecting rationality, which is, however, constrained by economic and social environment (Parada, 2005). In turn, NIE promotes the idea of individuals not being utility-maximisers but subjected to "bounded rationality"; individual being "intendedly rational, but only limitedly so" (Simon, 1961).

The mainstream of NIE is not homogeneous and there are a few complementary theories that are part of it, like agency theory, transaction costs and property rights theory (Kim and Mahoney, 2005). The most important aspect of the agency theory is basing it on the agency relationship that engages two parties – the principal and the agent. The agency relationship is a contract under which the principal delegates work to the agent to perform it on their behalf (Jensen and Meckling, 1976; Eisenhardt, 1989). The agent receives gratification for their performance as long as it meets the principal's expectations and interests. However, there is opportunism in the agency relationship – both parties of this relationship have different aims and risk preferences. In turn, the theory of transaction costs is premised on the idea that the boundaries of the organisation depend not only on the productive technology, but also on the costs of transacting business (Coase, 1937). The decision to organise transactions within the firm as opposed to on the open market (the "make and buy decision") depends on the relative costs of internal and external exchanges (Coase, 1937; Williamson, 1975, 1985; Hart and Moore, 1990). The market mechanism entails certain costs related, e.g., discovering relevant prices, negotiating and enforcing contracts. Within the firm, the entrepreneur can reduce these transaction costs by coordinating activities regarding contractual commitments by themselves. However, the internal organisation also generates another type of costs related to information flows, incentives, monitoring and performance evaluation. The nature of the firm is, thus, determined by the relative costs of organising transactions under alternative institutional arrangements. As far as the property rights theory is concerned, it assumes that the production and consumption of goods and services have an impact on market participants. In other words, there are externalities in each economy. Due to the internalisation of externalities, the range of unexchangeable relations can be reduced; however, it is connected with transaction costs (securing property rights has its price). The main task of the government should be ensuring the accurate division of property rights. They are defined by formal economic rules, whereas political decision-making specifies and enforces them. As Klein (2000) argued, NIE has been particularly interested in contract law and property rights; however, to the contrary of the traditional approach that disputes are preliminarily settled by courts as the official agents of the state, this mainstream often focuses on private solutions. In many cases, the parties of a dispute can produce more satisfactory solutions than professionals (e.g., judges, lawyers) that are constrained by the application of general rules of law on the basis of limited knowledge about the dispute (Galanter, 1981).

An interest in institutions and institutional environment has increasingly grown in the history of economics and enriched the perception and comprehension of its development through time. Whereas economic development was initially regarded as a gradual, inevitable transformation from local autarky to specialisation and division of labour, contemporarily it is perceived as response to the evolution of institutions that facilitate social and commercial relations. Thus, economic growth depends on the degree to which potential risks related to the trade exchange (e.g., decreasing) can be controlled and managed by institutions, which reduce information costs, encourage capital formation and mobility and allow for risks to be reduced and shared; in other words, they facilitate cooperation. Hence, NIE emphasises the significance of effective institutions as the main factors of economic growth and development.

Summing up the considerations on institutionalisation, it is worth emphasising several features and objectives, which accompany multilateral cooperation. First, institutionalisation aims at setting common norms of social coexistence, which is reflected, among others, in the introduction of common international conventions, regulating different areas of relations among states. Second, it strives for achieving important goals, common for the specified group of states or the whole international community, such as economic and social development, international security, protection of natural environment, health protection, etc. Third, it helps prevent common threats, such as armed aggression, terrorism, organised crime, illegal drug trafficking, trafficking in persons, etc. Moreover, institutionalisation is to promote common values, such as democracy, the rule of law, human rights and minority rights. Last but not least, it aims at preventing natural disasters (earthquakes, floods, droughts) and combating their effects. Actually, the role of institutions and institutional environment in the world economy is hard to overestimate, since institutions, in connection with the economic policy and spatial location, determine the level of the country's economic development.

2.3 Institutional forms and models of economic integration

Economic integration (international or supranational) may take different forms determined by the geographical or institutional criterion. With regard to the geographical criterion, economic integration can embrace a number of countries limited to a region or sub-region (i.e., regional integration) or unlimited number of countries (i.e., global integration). From the institutional perspective, economic integration can be divided into simple forms (enabling the move of goods and services) and complex forms (additionally enabling the movement of production factors and also fostering the creation of new ties/relations).

Balassa (1962) argued that economic integration may undergo certain stages of advancement, and distinguished its five forms, representing a varying degree:

- free trade area,
- customs union (CU),
- common market (CM),

- economic union,
- complete economic integration.

A free trade area is based on the abolishment of tariffs (and quantitative restrictions) between participating countries; however, each country keeps its own tariff barriers in trade with non-members. An example is the North American Free Trade Agreement formed in 1993 by the USA, Canada and Mexico. A CU assumes, apart from the suppression of discrimination in the area of commodity movements within the union, the introduction of equal tariffs in trade with non-member countries. These common external tariffs may differ across goods, but not across the participating countries.[6] The European Community formed in 1957 by West Germany, France, Italy, Belgium, the Netherlands and Luxembourg can serve as an example. A higher form of integration then those mentioned above is a CM, which enables a free movement of goods and services as well as a free migration of labour and capital among member states, usually referred to as factor integration. At the beginning of 1993, the European Union (EU) achieved the form of a CM. An economic union combines the suppression of restrictions on commodity and factor movement with a certain degree of the harmonisation of economic, monetary (an essential element of an economic union is the introduction of a single currency), tax and social policies of member states. This is usually referred to as "policy integration". The most advanced form of an economic integration could be a monetary union, e.g., EU members who use a single currency, the euro. Finally, complete economic integration means integration, as a result of which a homogenous area is created with political and economic institutions, whose decisions are binding for all member states. This form assumes the complete unification of economic, social, financial and legal policies.

The forms of economic integration distinguished by Balassa are quoted most frequently in the literature; however, it is also worth presenting the typology introduced by other scholars. For example, Tinbergen (1965) sought three forms of economic integration:

- exchange of goods without capital and people transfers,
- trade in goods, capital transfers only,
- trade in goods as well as capital and people transfer.

Molle (2001, pp. 10–12) distinguished between several forms of economic integration, subsequently occurring at the market level and at the level of the economic policy:

- free trade area, focusing on the abolishment of quotas and tariffs among trading partners.
- Incomplete CU, which introduces common external tariffs among member states; however, with respect to certain goods and services, trade barriers are still maintained.

- CU, implementing common tariffs for trade with other countries outside the union.
- Incomplete CM, whose first element is CU. On this market there is a free movement of substantial segments of labour and capital.
- CM, which enables a free movement of goods, services as well as production factors (labour and capital).
- Economic union, meaning the coordination of economic, monetary, tax, social and environmental policies of member states.
- Monetary union, in which the currencies of individual member states are interconnected by means of fixed exchange rates, or a single currency for all countries of the union is introduced.
- Economic and monetary union, combining the features of the economic and monetary union, which is characterised by a high degree of coherence between macroeconomics and budget policies.
- Politic union, where integration is extended to the sphere of politics.
- Full union, meaning the full integration of the economies of the integrating countries and common policies. As a consequence, the single area with political and economic institutions is established, whose decisions are binding for member states.

Similarly, Misala (2005) perceived integration as a process occurring at two levels, thus differentiating two forms (components) of economic integration – real integration and institutional–instrumental integration. The real component of integration is based on strengthening relations among individual actors of international relations and economic entities, such as households, enterprises, multinational corporations, society, intergovernmental and intragovernmental organisations, as well as national economies. At the country's level it means unifying national economic potentials in one changing potential and international organism, which is distinguished from the entire world economy. Such distinguished sub-system of the world economy is characterised by a high degree of reciprocal economic ties in terms of production, trade, science and technology. In turn, the institutional–instrumental component of integration is constituted by the economic policy, which drives economic integration. This component is based on the realisation of a specific form of integration while fostering its effectiveness, thus proceeding to its higher stage (e.g., free trade area, CU, CM, currency union, political union) and utilising diversified instruments and institutions to achieve the full form of economic (including monetary) and political integration. Simultaneously, if the institutional–instrumental component surpasses the real component, then the concept of politically driven integration is realised. However, if the real component surpasses the institutional–instrumental component, then the regional integration is driven by economic factors. However, for different reasons (e.g., the requirement of technological progress and economic development embodied by increasing and rapidly diversifying demand), at a certain level of economic development, the particular point of the intensity of regional integration is surpassed – the point of no return – when the top-down (institutional–instrumental) management of integration, regarding the flows of products and production factors, is inevitable.

In the literature, two basic models of economic integration are usually presented – the model of international economic integration and the model of supranational economic integration. The first group embraces free trade area and CU. It is based on the mechanism of free market and trade. The role of the state is limited to the protection of free market and trade within the state or integrating grouping. The second group of models embraces supranational models of economic integration, including CM, monetary union, economic union and full economic integration. In turn, the model of supranational integration is characterised by the unification of the market mechanism with state interventionism. In this case particular member states as well as the supranational institution are entitled to influence the integration process. Scott (1999) also introduced a mixed model of economic integration, which includes the elements typical of both models discussed above. The practice of European integration can be defined as a process of moving from the model of international integration to the model of supranational integration. Nowadays, we deal with federalisation of the EU – the process when the EU is transforming from confederation (the union of sovereign states) into federation (one federal states with the central government, comprising partially autonomous federal states).

To the already complex group of trade arrangements, there should also be added a set of combinations that result from different interactions among countries participating in them. Lipsey (1991) outlined three distinct models to describe these situations. The first model – the "hub-and-spoke" model, studied by Wonnacott (1990) – considers the case, in which a country has separate bilateral (or plurilateral) free trade agreements (FTAs) with a group of countries that do not have trade agreements among themselves. In this way, the "hub" enjoys free (or preferential) access to the market of the "spokes", while each of them can have free access only to the market of the "hub" and is prevented from realising gains with other "spokes". The second model – the overlapping regional free trade model – describes the situation that derives from an "original" bilateral FTA to which subsequent trade agreements are added by means of negotiations comprising only one of the "original" partners and different third countries, producing as a result that each of the former is included in some agreements while excluded from others. Krissoff and Sharples (1993) pointed out that the difficulty in enforcing an overlapping FTA may be high, particularly in aspects related with the flow of goods across trade areas and the application of the rules of origin. Finally, in the plurilateral regional model, several countries establish FTAs in which all member countries have (and permit) access to all markets.

Following the considerations presented above, it can be concluded that market integration, referring to goods, services and production factor markets, is mainly connected to international exchange, foreign investment and labour migration. Its basis is the liberalisation of trade and investment, i.e., removing market barriers, constraining the freedom of transfers as well securing the conditions of free competition in the integrated area. In turn, the second form of integration – integration of politics – concerns different fields of the economic policy. Different forms of cooperation among national governments and supranational institutions aim to fulfil tasks belonging to the sphere of the economic policy. Integration of politics may take various forms, ranging from information and counselling to coordination, harmonisation and unification. Its degree is diverse at different phases of the integration process. In principle, lower stages require weaker integration of politics, whereas higher stages reflect stronger integration of governments' actions. Thus, it can be stated that lower phases are characterised by "negative integration", which mainly deals with removing obstacles for the free movement of goods, services and production factors. In turn, at higher phases, "positive integration" proceeds, i.e., national governments cooperate with each other, eliminating market distortions. Positive integration entails the creation of new forms of institutions ensuring effective public interventions, which means, in practice, the necessity to pass national governments' competences to supranational institutions or to establish new institutions equipped with specific entitlements. As a consequence, deepening integration of politics justifies the development of supranational institutions and drives supranational economic integration.

It is also worth stressing that there is a common belief in the literature that economic integration should take an institutional form; i.e., it should be based on international institutions, which initiate, supervise and coordinate the integration process occurring among integrating countries. As a matter of fact, in the majority of cases, the contemporary economic integration takes place in a form of international groupings. However, there are exceptions in this matter; e.g., the integration between the USA and Canada, which was realised for many years not in an institutional form. The same applies to the Nordic integration during the first half of the 20th century. Also, East Asian integration pursued without any institutional structures until the late 1990s, when the institutionalisation process began. However, the establishment of integration institutions does not necessarily mean that the integration process proceeds in their frameworks; sometimes the integration process occurred within them is solely of a symbolic character. In practice, this phenomenon was proved by a number of African and Latin American integration institutions, e.g., East African Community, CU in Africa, Economic Community of the Great Lakes Countries, Latin American Free Trade Association and Latin American Integration Association.

Notes

1 The text of the speech can be found on https://rm.coe.int/16806981f3 (accessed: 05.04.2024).

2 The text of the speech can be found on https://www.oecd.org/general/themarshall-planspeechatharvarduniversity5june1947.htm (accessed: 05.04.2024).

3 The text of the statement can be found on https://www.cvce.eu/en/obj/statement_by_paul_hoffman_at_the_75th_oeec_council_meeting_31_october_1949-en-840d9b55-4d17-4c33-8b09-7ea547b85b40.html (accessed: 05.04.2024).

4 Point XIV of the Fourteen Points; see Hofstadter and Hofstadter (1982).

5 Churchill advocated the creation of the United States of Europe in a speech of 1949 in Zürich; see Cannadine (1990).

6 For more see: GATT, Par. 8, art. XXIV; https://www.wto.org/english/tratop_e/region_e/region_art24_e.htm (accessed: 08.04.2024).

3 East Asian model of regional economic integration – ascendants, evolution and outcomes

East Asia's regional economic integration was mainly market-driven; East Asian economies promoted trade and investment liberalisation, which in turn resulted in a rapid regional economic growth, curbing further liberalisation. Subsequently, these phenomena fostered integration processes in East Asia, and rapidly growing East Asian economies became both the sources and destinations of international trade and foreign direct investment (FDI). Consequently, this market-driven economic integration has gradually been complemented by an institution-driven element in East Asia. This chapter analysis the specificity of East Asia's economic integration and the role of multinational corporation in these processes. Additionally, the function of Association of Southeast Asian Nations (ASEAN) and Asia Pacific Economic Cooperation (APEC) in the evolution of institutionalised regionalism in East Asia. Finally, the major outcomes of institutionalising East Asia's economic integration in a form of the establishment of regional and region-wide free trade agreements (FTAs) are presented.

3.1 Specificity of East Asia's economic integration against the European background

In terms of specifically perceived anthropomorphism, it can be argued that if cooperation among states is the product of nature, then the forms that institutionalisation takes are usually the work of culture. States, while making the decision about cooperation, reject an alternative choice, which is isolation. This choice is made on the basis of the profit and loss account, resulting from such cooperation. In the case of choosing isolation, the advantages from cooperation are relatively small, whereas the level of risk connected to opening to a potential partner is high. The acceptance of partnership or alliance reflects, in fact, the expectations of relatively large benefits. In long-term activities, states usually avoid risky behaviour. Therefore, they aim at minimising threats and maximising benefits. Such a choice between isolation and openness depends, amongst other, on the mono- or multi-culturalism of a given nation, the system of values as well as the social and political systems. It can be assumed that

DOI: 10.4324/9781003544234-3

liberal and democratic states of open and market economies are more willing to cooperate. The choice of organising the society in both the inter- and intra-state system is embodied by two opposite models – the model of subordination (the imperial model) and the model of cooperation (the co-ordinational model). The choice of the model is determined by the configuration of power in the society. Imbalance fosters the imperial model, whereas relative parity favours/enforces cooperation. It is also influenced by cultural patterns, among others, the state's propensity to repeat experiences of internal relations in the external ones.

In the context of globalising world economy, the end of the Cold War and often lack of economic and political stability were strong incentives for economic cooperation for countries characterised by diverse economic structures and different level of economic development, usually neighbouring trading partners. Just like the domino effect, when countries integrated in one region to realise the shared economic interests, other regions also started implementing the same process. Towards the end of the second wave of globalisation, at the turn of the 1980s and the 1990s, economic integration constituted its integral part and some similarities of integration processes in different regions worldwide could be observed. However, on the other hand, integration in North America, Asia or Africa substantially differed and had many diverse features. Under the third wave of globalisation, the liberalisation model, in which institutionalisation East Asian countries also participate, has been changed. Since, previously, East Asian economies took part mainly in bilateral (and multilateral) non-discriminatory trade liberalisation, nowadays a great number of integration agreements exist in the region, leading to the creation of a complex system of ties, which are relatively shallow, often initiated bottom-up and connected to political cooperation. However, since the second half of the 21st century, a new wave of East Asian regionalism has been observed – East Asian "loose" regionalism has been complemented by its "tighter" form, which can be reflected in the establishment of two regional institutional arrangements: the Comprehensive and Progressive Agreement for Trans-Pacific Partnership (CPTPP) and the Regional Comprehensive Economic Partnership (RCEP).

The pattern of East Asian integration does not indicate the feature of strong institutionalisation, which is typical of the European model of regional integration. Also, it does not replicate the pattern of economic integration with a dominating economy, which takes place, for example, in North America. In the literature, we can also encounter such a view that economic relations among East Asian countries are difficult to unambiguously classify to regionalism or regionalisation. Many initiatives in terms of financial, monetary, trade or military cooperation require a certain degree of institutionalisation, which is indispensable for their implementation and coordination. Nevertheless, East Asian economies, in contrast to Europeans, have not shown clear determination to establish strong supranational institutions.

There are several reasons for differences in perceiving the universalism of regional integration by European and East Asian countries. It may largely arise from the fact that Asia, in contrast to Europe, is the region of many civilisations. Asian societies are characterised by the coexistence of collectivism with the multiplicity of traditions. On one hand, these are societies possessing individual ownership and deriving human rights and freedoms, but on the other hand, these are also authoritarian societies of depersonalised ownership. Additionally, these societies have a totally different past, and currently are confronted with the state of international affairs, in which one hyperpower prevails and the universalisation of one cultural model proceeds. However, the Asian culture has not been familiar with such a state of affairs, which, may also justify the lack of the institutions of cooperation in the region, analogical to contemporary institutions typical of Europe or other parts of the world.

As a matter of fact, the cause of unwillingness or inability to create a strong institutional framework in East Asia can be also sought in the lack of the broadly understood cohesiveness of the region, reflected in all aspects of its functioning. This embraces differences in the size of territory and population as well as ethnic, religious (almost all the world's religions are present), linguistic, systemic (constitutional monarchies, democratic republics, communist countries and military dictatorships coexist) and social differences (e.g., in the level of education, life expectancy). These existing diversities do not foster setting common objectives and arriving at the form of cooperation suitable and beneficial for all countries in the region.

Additionally, East Asian countries are characterised by substantial differences in the level of economic development, concepts of trade and economic cooperation (Próchniak and Suska, 2023; Suska, 2023). Spectacular achievements in terms of economic growth and equity of East Asian countries, especially Japan and the Asian Tigers, can be attributed to the varieties of capitalism (VoC) (Moore, 2018; Lee, 2020; Lee and Shin, 2021). Hall and Soskice's (2001) study on VoC identified two representative types of capitalism – liberal market economies (LMEs) and coordinated market economies (CMEs), providing an important way to understand and compare economic systems worldwide. The scholars focused on how firms enter into a relationship with other actors, such as workers suppliers, business associations, governments and other stakeholders. If firms mainly use market institutions, such as competitions and formal contracts, the economy is then classified as LME, e.g., the US, the UK, Australia, Canada, New Zealand and Ireland. If firms use a non-market relationship, such as a strategic interaction among actors as a form of coordination, the economy is classified as CME, e.g., Germany, Japan, Switzerland, the Netherlands, Belgium, Sweden, Norway, Denmark, Finland and Austria. In turn, France, Italy, Spain, Portugal, Greece and Turkey are perceived as mixed market economies given their ambiguous position. Soskice and Hall (2001) argued that each type of capitalism is stable and efficient in terms of its economic performance, owing to complementarity among its institutional components. Although LMEs and CMEs have different institutions in economic, political and social areas, they both can be efficient with comparative institutional advantage. East Asian economy was considered a manufacturing-oriented economy in the past. However, the share of financial sectors in the economies in these countries has rapidly increased since the 1980s. Structural changes accompanied by increasing financialisation in East Asia could justify convergence between the Anglo-Saxon and East Asian capitalism (characterised by high growth and low inequality). The situation in continental Europe may differ due to its long history of capitalism. Thus, institutional complementarity and path dependency are stronger in Europe than in East Asia. Therefore, European countries may be capable of maintaining their own types of capitalism and their specific institutions, particularly labour market institutions rather than converge to Anglo-Saxon capitalism. Hence, the character of East Asia's integration can be widely explained by the VoC, which provide a useful framework for explaining variation in the types of governance institutions that appear in developing countries. It is argued that additional "veto players" increase the likelihood of having a coordinated rather than liberal economic system. Together, the number of "veto players" and the level of systemic vulnerability are expected to influence economic governance institutions by shaping the policy environment and thus the micro incentives facing workers, investors and managers (Moore, 2018).

To the catalogue of the reasons for institutional weakness in East Asia, additionally, strong dependence on other world's regions, especially on the USA and its focus on bilateral relationships as opposed to multilateral frameworks, can be added. This situation imposed the necessity to consider concepts of the regional development strategy, which did not necessarily correlate with the specificity as well as the social and political characters of the region, dominated by general reluctance to establishing rigid top-down institutions, overtaking certain competences of states (Katzenstein, 2005). Hence, the form of institutionalisation embraced by East Asia is different than, for example, in Europe and it allows for East Asian adherence to the principle of non-intervention into domestic affairs, the dominant emphasis on national interests and the manner of elitism.

While comparing East Asia's regional integration with other models of integration, especially in Europe, the distinction between two forms of integration – market-driven integration (regionalisation) and institution-driven integration (regionalism) – should be highlighted. Dent (2017) distinguished between integration at the micro-level steadily progressing in East Asia since 1960s, driven by market forces (like regional production networks and multinational enterprises [MNEs]), based on voluntary/unilateral liberalisation of trade and investment, which has been supplemented by integration at the macro-level. The latter has been pursued since the 1990s, when East Asian countries began to search for strengthening regional cooperation at the intergovernmental level. In contrast to East Asia, in Europe, we find economic

Table 3.1 East Asian versus European model of regional integration

Region	*East Asia*	*Europe*
Type of regional integration	Market-driven integration	Functional and institutional integration
Foundations of integration processes	Soft institutions, open regionalism, non-binding decision-making, flexible consensus	Treaties and legally binding commitments
Driving forces of integration processes	MNCs	National politicians, European union bureaucrats
Role of the government in integration processes	Facilitator	Leader
Character of trade	Focused on the world market, but growing significance of intra-regional trade	Focused on intra-regional trade
Character of investment	Production networks	Dense links
Monetary integration	Still weak	Tight (Euro)

Source: Own elaboration.

integration with the regional institutional arrangement of the European Union (EU). The foundation of European integration is treaties and legally binding commitments, whereas East Asian countries show rather a non-legalistic approach to intergovernmental cooperation, which is based on soft institutions, cooperative security, non-binding decision-making, convention and consensus-building (Dosch and Dent, 2012). Nevertheless, Soestro (2006, p. 230) argued that East Asian market-driven integration, as summarised in Table 3.1, "has stepped into the area of institutional cooperation and integration led by national governments". The proliferation of FTAs in the region under no common regime has urged them to step up their role from "facilitators to more proactive participants of the integration process". Hence, it can be concluded that East Asia's economic integration embraces the elements of market-driven regionalisation, which has gradually been complemented by institutionalised regionalism. It seems that they both fit the East Asian cooperative framework and the specificity of the region.

3.2 The role of multinational enterprises in East Asian integration processes

One of the most distinctive features of East Asian economic integration is that it was largely market-driven, with trade and investment as its main driving forces as well as with MNEs as its main driving actors. Japan first emerged as a regional exporter in the 1960s, followed by Hong Kong, South Korea, Singapore and Taiwan in the 1970s. The development of the export-growth strategy was accompanied by the change in the export structure from basic commodities to capital intensive products. Since the 1980s East Asian countries have undergone a shift from labour intensive commodities to high technology products, which was reflected in a decrease in exports of textile and agricultural products together with a rapid increase in exports of machinery products (Pornjantuek et al., 2020). Over the last decades, e.g., between 1997 and 2021, the region's share in world exports expanded from 25% to 34%, while its imports rose from 24% to 30% of world imports. The expansion of international trade has been accompanied by a substantial growth in intra-regional trade. It was particularly relevant for Southeast Asian countries (especially ASEAN countries). In the period 1997–2012, the share of intra-ASEAN exports in total exports increased from 23% to 26%, whereas intra-ASEAN imports increased from 18% to 22% of total imports. Intra-regional trade with Northeast Asian economies has been less intense, which results from the fact that China, but also Japan and South Korea, has largely been dependent on extra-regional trade (Suska, 2023).

The extensive trade cooperation in the region was driven by MNEs, which – as the major foreign traders and investors – played a significant role in East Asian integration (Pempel, 2005; Soesastro, 2006; Urata, 2009; Yang and Huang, 2011) in contrast to, e.g., the EU associated with extensive political structures. MNEs established regional production networks to boost the production efficiency, which became one of the most significant mechanisms of creating strong ties among highly diversified economies in the region, simultaneously contributing to an increase in the number of East Asian countries participating integration. A number of interconnected processes have prepared the regional environment to the creation of these regional production networks, initiated in the mid-1980s after the Plaza Accord. Regional economies with a different level of economic development (like e.g., East Asian economies) are characterised by varied costs and availability of production factors. Therefore, global businesses locate particular modules of production networks in different locations (within and outside the region), utilising local comparative advantages. The technological progress in transportation, information and communication enables more effective management of production networks at a distance from the enterprises' headquarters. Since it is essential to combine the subsequent stages of production into a single whole, the interdependencies of integrating economies (also those outside the region) are becoming stronger. As a consequence of this bottom-up process, interests in tighter international cooperation at the political level are increasing. Also, host governments are pressed to compete with each other for FDI as well as production factors, like individual talent and capital, as an important engine for economic growth and development. Simultaneously, they are pushed by various global institutions, e.g., the World Trade Organisation (WTO) and the International Monetary Fund (IMF), to liberalise their economies (for more see, e.g., Munakata, 2004; Soesastro, 2006).

Urata (2009) argued that the emergence of regional productional networks especially in electronics and electric machinery promoted economic integration in East Asia. The author emphasised the region's role as a world factory for these commodities as East Asian countries produced finished products by assembling parts supplied from developing and developed economies and sold them in world markets. Such regional production networks were formed mainly by MNEs from Japan, the USA and the EU, as they fragmented the production process into various sub-processes and located them in a country or region where they could be conducted most effectively through FDI. MNEs adopted this fragmentation, taking advantage of substantial diversity of the level of economic development and wages among East Asian countries.

Especially, Japanese MNEs played a leading role in the initial stages of East Asian economic integration, when they established the region-wide production and distribution network, resulting in a multi-tier division of labour with production processes relocated to low-cost assembly services, which shaped the pattern of trade and industrialisation in East Asia (Okita, 1991). This pattern corresponded with the Akamatsu's "flying geese" model, with Japan as the "lead goose", which industrialised first, and was followed by East Asian newly industrialised economies (NIEs) and finally by ASEAN countries. Akamatsu attempted to explain the catching-up process of industrialisation in latecomer economies, identifying, through the statistical analysis of Japan's industrial development before the World War II, two patterns, which looked like a flying geese formation: (1) a basic pattern, in which a single industry grows tracing out the three successive curves of imports, production and exports; and (2) a variant pattern, in which industries are diversified and upgraded from consumer goods to capital goods and/or from simple to more advanced products. In his post-war works, Akamatsu added a third pattern of intercountry alignment in order to explain the regional and international transmission of "flying geese" development from a lead goose to follower geese, according to which the consumer goods industry becomes already homogenised and attains the same standard with that of the advanced countries. Therefore, they are no longer less-advanced countries in the consumer goods industry. Subsequently, this advanced status is further developed; however, in this stage, exports of these consumer goods begin to decline. It results from the fact that they are put into production in other less-advanced countries and development in a "flying geese" pattern is under way. Additionally, capital goods domestically produced begin to be exported; hence, in place of decreasing exports of consumer goods, capital goods are exported and reach the stage of high-degree heterogeneity in regard to other less-advanced countries. Following this sequence, underdeveloped nations are aligned successively behind advanced industrial nations in a "flying geese" pattern (Kojima, 2000).

Growing outward direct investment from Japan from the mid-1980s as well as from NIEs from the 1990s to the rest of the region increased the flow of raw materials and intermediate goods within manufacturing networks in

East Asia, fuelling a rise in intra-regional trade (Barrell and Choy, 2003). In turn, for ASEAN countries, the spurt of growth began with the relocation of Japanese enterprises, followed by those of NIEs. However, while Japanese enterprises initially relocated part of their production facilities in Taiwan, Singapore and Hong Kong, rising costs in Japan and in the mentioned NIEs due to the strengthening of yen in the wake of the 1985 Plaza Agreement, simultaneously to ASEAN's relatively low labour and production costs, prompted the diversion of FDI flows toward ASEAN. Also, stable macroeconomic environment and the increased liberalisation of ASEAN countries were pull factors not only for Japan but also for NIEs, which started to locate their investments in new low-cost sites (Nicolas, 2010). The inflow of new production facilities enabled the receiving ASEAN countries to grow at a faster pace and to further liberalise their trade.

The character of industrialisation and trade in East Asia, following the "flying geese" model, contributed to deeper functional integration of trade, production and technology linkages that have been forged by MNEs and other forms of transnational business activity in the region. These processes were largely intensified during globalisation, especially as a result of trade and investment liberalisation. Gradually, the significance of the region of East Asia has been growing in global economy and the production hub of the contemporary world economy has been shifting towards East Asian markets.

3.3 The function of ASEAN and APEC in institutionalising regional economic integration

In the evolution of East Asia's institutionalised economic integration, ASEAN and APEC played a significant role. In this process several phases can be highlighted. Munakata (2004) argued that the first period started in the mid-1980s and was related to the creation of APEC and ASEAN Free Trade Area (AFTA) as well as various competitive proposals for regional cooperation. The first impetus for institutionalising economic integration in the region came from the USA in a form of a proposal to create ASEAN-US FTA. However, ASEAN was not fully prepared to address this challenge, then. Subsequently, in the late 1980s, the USA came up with an idea of bilateral FTAs with Japan, South Korea and Taiwan. Australia and Japan also considered the creation of a regional framework for economic cooperation, the APEC, although, initially, the Australian proposal did not consider either Canada or the USA. Only under pressure from Japan, these two states were also invited for the first, official meeting of foreign ministers in Canberra in 1989. Then, the participating countries – Australia, New Zealand, Japan, South Korea, the USA, Canada and six ASEAN countries (Brunei, Indonesia, Malaysia, the Philippines, Singapore and Thailand) – decided that APEC, in the first stage, should be an informal forum for discussion regarding economic matters at governmental level, whereas the issues concerning APEC's structure and expansion by new members were postponed (US Department of State, 1998). During the first years of APEC, it established the core objectives, and gradually expanded the range of its activities and functions. APEC members proclaimed the creation of a liberalised FTA in the Asia-Pacific as well as ten working groups were established as regular features to develop activities, contributing to the achievement of APEC's objectives. In 1991, APEC expanded membership by the admission of China, Hong Kong and Taiwan. In the subsequent year, the permanent Secretariat was established to facilitate APEC's cooperation, as well as the Eminent Person Group was also appointed to enunciate the action plan and APEC's vision for regional trade by 2000 (Quimba and Barral, 2019).

Consequently, ASEAN, concerned about the threat of a possible loss of its bargain power with the strengthening of APEC's position and about the inflow of competitive FDI from Eastern Europe and China, launched in 1992 a new regional economic initiative – the AFTA to facilitate intra-regional trade of East Asian countries. When the AFTA agreement was originally signed, ASEAN embraced six members – Brunei, Indonesia, Malaysia, the Philippines, Singapore and Thailand. Vietnam officially joined ASEAN and also AFTA in 1995, Laos and Myanmar in 1997 and Cambodia in 1999. It is worth mentioning that ASEAN's first attempts towards open and flexible approach to trade liberalisation in the region were made already in 1977, with the establishment of the ASEAN Preferential Trading Agreement (ASEAN PTA), which aimed to facilitate trade by allowing trade preferences on the product-by-product basis (Bende-Nabende, 1999). Over the years, the list of products embraced by liberalisation was enlarged and non-tariff barriers were decreased. Although ASEAN PTA was quite impressive in terms of the number of the items covered, their impact on intra-ASEAN trade was rather minimal. Despite the fact that each country undertook to expand the specified number of preferences on regular basis, they were not on products, which had a significant share in the trade exchange within ASEAN. Additionally, the positive effects of ASEAN PTA were largely reduced because of national exclusion lists of products, which were to protect the national industry from foreign competition. Moreover, the products covered by preferences were often either low valued or other versions of the same product, or not subject to the trade exchange at all. As a result, the share of goods covered by preferences eventually accounted for only 2% of intra-ASEAN trade at the beginning of the 1980s (Chng, 1985).

AFTA, to enhance economic cooperation and trade liberalisation, implemented the Common Effective Preferential Tariff scheme, which was perceived as a vehicle for intra-ASEAN tariff liberalisation, removing quantitative restrictions and other non-tariff barriers. Under the scheme, for goods originating within ASEAN, the member countries were to apply a tariff rate of 0–5. ASEAN members agreed to enact zero tariff rates on virtually all imports by 2010 for the original signatories – the ASEAN-6 (i.e., Brunei, Indonesia,

Malaysia, the Philippines, Singapore and Thailand) and by 2015 for the CLMV countries (i.e., Cambodia, Laos, Myanmar and Vietnam).

Simultaneously, with the incorporation of China, Taiwan and Hong Kong into APEC, the USA renewed its interests in opening up East Asian markets through this integration grouping, which began the transition to the second phase of the development of East Asia's institutionalised economic integration. It started in 1993, when the USA chaired APEC, and ended in 1997 with the outbreak of the Asian financial crisis and was characterised by APEC's primacy as the main engine for regional cooperation under strong US leadership. As a result, several significant decisions were made, such as: (1) the consent to admit Mexico and Papua New Guinea to APEC; (2) commitment to organising meetings of finance ministers to expand APEC's cooperation in the area of international finance and (3) elaborating plans of the practical fulfilment of APEC's objectives and visions by three existing bodies, i.e., Working Groups, Pacific Business Forum and Committee on Trade and Investment (CTI). Another milestone in the period of APEC's dominance was issuing, in 1994, the APEC Economic Leaders' Declaration of Common Resolve (known as the Bogor Declaration), including the Bogor Goals, which committed the APEC countries to create conditions for trade and investment liberalisation in the region by 2020. Consequently in 1995, three main pillars of APEC were established: (1) trade and investment liberalisation; (2) trade facilitation and (3) economic and technical cooperation, with the Osaka Action Agenda. Also, APEC CTI elaborated the so-called "1996 Work Programmes" concerning a number of issues, like tariffs/non-tariff measures, tariff database, investment, customs procedures, standards and conformance, competition policy/deregulation, government procurement, dispute mediation, mobility of business people, intellectual property rights, implementation of the Uruguay Round, rules of origin, services, information gathering and analysis and trade policy dialogue. Additionally, in 1996, the Manila Action Plan was adopted, which provided the guidelines for achieving the Bogor Goals by 2010 and 2020 through trade and investment liberalisation, including the creation of the APEC Business Advisory Council, which recognised the significant role of the business sector for APEC's work and success.

However, regardless of numerous achievements, APEC turned rather ineffective in fulfilling the most expectations of its members since, in fact, it attached a lower priority to economic cooperation. However, despite the fact that APEC did not manage to solve all the issues relevant for that period, it drove integration in East Asia, bringing national governments and businesses together through many meetings and projects as well as making them aware of common problems, new channels of cooperation and diverse priorities in the region. Additionally, the establishment of APEC together with rapid economic growth in East Asia stimulated European interests in the region, which resulted in the Asia Europe Meeting in the mid-1990s.

During the second phase of institutionalising economic integration in East Asia, also ASEAN was active in the region's cooperative framework. In response to progressing integration processes all over the world (e.g., the EU, NAFTA) as well as exceeding traditional free trade in goods to also cover services and investments, ASEAN, besides AFTA, undertook further initiatives to foster intra-regional economic cooperation. As a result, the ASEAN Framework Agreement on Services (AFAS) and the Framework Agreement on the ASEAN Investment Area (AIA) were established in 1995 and 1998, respectively. Under the AFAS, services liberalisation covered such areas as business services, professional services, construction, distribution, education, environment services, health care, maritime transport, telecommunication and tourism. ASEAN also created regional frameworks for professional services, like, e.g., engineering, architecture, accountancy, medical and dental practitioners and nursing services. In turn, AIA covered such sectors as manufacturing, agriculture, fisheries, forestry and mining and services incidental to these sectors. Additionally, ASEAN introduced the ASEAN Industrial Cooperation (AICO) scheme in 1996 to promote joint manufacturing between ASEAN-based companies; e.g., AICO has successfully facilitated production networks in the automobile and electronic industries (Yoshimatsu, 2002).

The 1997 Asian financial crisis initiated another phase in the institutionalisation of economic integration in the region. It envisaged the East Asian nations' different issues that prompted them to initiate regional cooperation. First, the experience of the crisis convinced the countries in East Asia that they had to protect their own interests because global institutions under US leadership (i.e., IMF) were not always reliable. Asian countries did not support the way the IMF, in conjunction with the US Treasury, addressed the crises, and they believed that global financial institutions even contributed to aggravating the hardships of the economies hit by the crisis. This perception, combined with the fact that the US hedge funds considerably profited from the massive disposing of Asian currencies, hampered the image of the USA in the region (Munakata, 2003). Secondly, the crisis destroyed regional domestic markets and focused the East Asian countries on trade outside the region. However, they were concerned about overcoming discriminations caused by FTAs that they did not belong to; hence, they started to seek trade agreements that would strengthen their relations with important world's markets. Third, the crisis envisaged the need for economic reform to attract FDI, which boosted the countries' interest in legally binding agreements with foreign countries. Moreover, in that period, the significance of ASEAN was undermined – China's relatively stable economic performance throughout the crisis as well as increased FDI flows into South Korea contrasted with the collapse of domestic demand and slow progress of economic reform in ASEAN. Finally, the Asian financial crisis resulted in a partial decrease of US interests in the region of East Asia. These experiences prompted East Asian countries to seek for regional cooperation to secure financial and economic stability in the region, which later shaped a more comprehensive idea of regional integration. Also, the change in the US attitude convinced the countries in the region that APEC should not be the only framework for regional cooperation, and they should seek for other alternatives (Munakata, 2006). Consequently, ASEAN countries as well as China, Japan and South Korea initiated the cooperation in the ASEAN+3 format, which was institutionalised in 1999, with the issue of the Joint Statement on East Asia Cooperation, confirming the establishment of a dialogue group – ASEAN Plus Three (APT). Consequently, APT finance ministers met in 2000 to discuss the creation of a regional financial framework, which eventually led to the adoption of the Chiang Mai Initiative. It started the development of a network of currency swap agreements as well as their further multilateralisation (Chiang Mai Initiative Multilateralization [CMIM]) in 2010. Such measures opened the way toward more proactive regional cooperation and integration in the financial and economic area. Soestro (2006) argued that East Asia's functional integration began with the establishment of the APT process in the wake of 1997/98 Asian financial crisis, which was regarded as the best vehicle for developing a strategy to develop with future crises. Indeed, in literature, the creation of APT is "widely regarded as an embryo of an East Asian cooperation arrangement. Some scholars speculate that it is the first step toward institutional integration in East Asia" (Soesastro, 2006, p. 231). Under the auspices of APT, the East Asia Vision Group, established in 1988, crafted out a vision of the cooperation toward regional community building. The "Towards an East Asian Community" report published in 2001 by EAVG and commissioned by APT member states noted that the Asian financial crisis envisaged the East Asian nation the necessity to institutionalise their cooperation to avoid future crises of that kind: "In particular, the Asian financial crisis of the recent past provided a strong impetus to strengthen regional cooperation. It has spurred the recognition that East Asia needs to institutionalise its cooperation to pre-empt or solve similar problems that may arise". The Group further envisaged

> East Asia moving from a region of nations to a bona fide community where collective efforts are made for peace, prosperity and progress. The economic field, including trade, investment and finance, is expected to serve as the catalyst in this community-building process.
>
> (EAVG, 2001)

The key recommendations of the report covered six areas of regional cooperation, including economic, financial and institutional cooperation. It is worth noting here that EAVG was established in the wake of Asian financial crisis and the report was published just after the crisis, so it had the influence on the recommendations included in the report. East Asian nations then felt the need to mutually cooperate in overcoming the crisis and as a result they institutionalised cooperation in different areas, including the economic-financial realms, and began building an East Asian community (EAVG, 2012). In turn, the East Asia Vision (EAVG) II Report on "Realising an East Asian Economic Community" published in 2012 proposed the establishment of "East Asian Economic Community" by 2020. Among the most important of the 59 recommendations provided in the report were negotiating RCEP, strengthening the existing regional financial governance mechanisms (e.g., CMIM), the creation of East Asian Monetary Fund and East Asia Infrastructural Investment Fund. While some of these recommendations have been realised, e.g., the establishment of RCEP, the core proposal of the creation of East Asian Economic Community in its entirety has not yet been formally adopted by APT members.

Taken into account the above considerations, a significant step regarding institutionalisation was taken with the vision of building the ASEAN Community, which was crafted in 2001 in the report published by EAVG. However, it should be here emphasised that the milestone in terms of East Asia's institutionalisation was launching the ASEAN Charter in 2007, which provided legally binding institutional framework and specified rules, norms, values, budget and finance, administrative procedures as well as the structure of institutional bodies (ASEAN, 2008). The Preamble of the Charter calls upon the ASEAN countries to respect the fundamental importance of the sovereignty of countries, reaffirming the principle of non-interference and consensus, and to adhere to democratic principles, the rule of law, good governance and human rights. It also reaffirms the commitment of ASEAN members in establishing a legal and institutional framework through the Charter and enhancing regional cooperation and integration through the establishment of an ASEAN Community comprising the ASEAN Security Community, the ASEAN Economic Community (AEC) and the ASEAN Socio-Cultural Community. The adoption of the ASEAN Charter is believed to transform ASEAN to become a more institutional organisation with principles and procedures to facilitate the process of disputes settlement and decision-making between the member countries. However, ASEAN countries were not very receptive with the concept of using consensus decision-making process to impose sanctions and changes. Therefore, a watered-down ASEAN Charter was adopted reflecting ASEAN's unreadiness to diverge away from the "ASEAN way" that had been realised over the past decades. Despite the addition of two new principles that touches on the collective responsibility and enhancing consultation, the ASEAN Charter still does not exhibit the transformation of ASEAN into a puissant organisation.

Since the turn of the millennium, East Asian countries have entered another stage in institutionalising economic integration related to the implementation of bilateral and multilateral FTAs. In the past, East Asian governments distanced themselves from PTAs, like FTAs, and did not peruse other formal institutions for regional integration; however, in the wake of the financial crisis, the situation substantially changed. Since then, East Asian countries started to actively explore bilateral and multilateral FTAs, aspiring to realise the vision of an "East Asian community of peace, prosperity and progress" (EAVG, 2001). Indeed, to boost trade and investment, many FTAs have been concluded in the region in recent years; AEC, CPTPP and RCEP are probably the most important ones among them. So far, the latter is the culmination of a decades-long pursuit of trade liberalisation and market integration within the world's economically most dynamic and most important region (Hilpert, 2022).

3.4 The proliferation of trade institutions in East Asia and the "noodle bowl" effect

The outcome of institutionalisation processes occurring in East Asia is a trading framework, characterised by a great number of bilateral and multilateral FTAs. The first Asian country, which triggered the trend for bilateral FTAs, was Japan. Its decision to conclude an FTA with Singapore in October 2000 accelerated other FTA negotiations in the region. Singapore was also actively seeking for the possibility for bilateral FTAs outside the region with, for example, the USA, Europe, China and India. The Singapore's declaration to negotiate a bilateral FTA with the USA in November 2000 prompted other ASEAN economies to explore FTAs with other countries.

China started to engage more actively in regional frameworks and considered an FTA with ASEAN after acceding WTO in 2000. China's positive experience of participating in APEC processes helped gradually overcome its fears that the multilateral framework could reduce its freedom and damage its interest. It began paying more attention to the region of East Asia, becoming a more confident and active actor. Consequently, China proposed establishing an FTA with all ten ASEAN economies and in 2002, they signed the Framework Agreement on the Comprehensive Economic Cooperation (CEC), as a legal instrument to govern future ASEAN-China economic cooperation. The Framework Agreement on CEC was supposed to establish a free trade area by 2010 for ASEAN-6 (Brunei, Indonesia, Malaysia, Philippines, Singapore and Thailand) and by 2015 for CLMV (Cambodia, Laos, Myanmar and Vietnam). In 2003, beginning with Thailand, China started to implement the early harvest programme to eliminate tariffs on some products (live animals, meat fish, diary produce, other animal products, live trees, vegetables, fruits and nuts) (Soesastro, 2005, 2006). However, some agricultural products, e.g., rice and palm oil, actually of great importance for ASEAN, were excluded from the programme. Negotiations on the FTA for goods beyond the early harvest programme were to be concluded by 2004 in frames of the Agreement on Trade in Goods of the Framework Agreement on CEC (ASEAN-China FTA [ACFTA]), followed by a series of agreements to implement the framework agreement.

Also, at the beginning of this millennium, Japan declared its interest in forming an Economic Partnership Agreement with ASEAN, including an FTA.

Consequently, Japan concluded its first FTA with Singapore (Japan-Singapore Partnership Agreement) and then with Malaysia, the Philippines, Thailand and Indonesia, moving towards the remaining ASEAN countries. Consequently, in 2003, ASEAN and Japan signed the Comprehensive Economic Partnership (CEP) with an FTA component to be completed within ten years. The agreement introduced several principles binding the member countries, like covering a wide range of sectors focusing on liberalisation, facilitation and cooperation activities; respecting integrity, solidarity and integration of ASEAN; consistency with the WTO rules; providing special and differential treatment to ASEAN countries with regard to their different levels of economic development, and additional flexibility to its newest members; addressing sensitive sectors in ASEAN countries and Japan with flexibility and consideration of technical cooperation and capacity building programmes (Soesastro, 2005, p. 9).

While negotiating FTAs with ASEAN, Japan adopted a dual strategy – with ASEAN as a grouping and selectively with individual ASEAN countries. Thus, the ASEAN-Japan CEP had a different character than the agreement between ASEAN and China (ACFTA). Namely, in ACFTA, ASEAN has become a "hub", whereas in ASEAN-Japan CEP, ASEAN countries serve as "spokes" in relation to Japan.

In turn, South Korea was initially reluctant to participate in bilateral FTA negotiations with ASEAN. Nevertheless, in 2004, the Joint Declaration on Comprehensive Cooperation was signed, and the ASEAN-Korea FTA (AKFTA) was created. While AKFTA was established later than other ASEAN's FTAs, the intention was to implement it earlier, and to fulfil a goal of achieving the level of liberalisation as high as possible. According to the agreement at least 80% of products should have zero tariffs in 2009, with consideration for special and differential treatment and additional flexibility for the CLMV countries.

The shift of the balance of power in East Asia caused by China's economic development, accompanied by its confident regional policy and Japan's stagnation attracted the attention of the USA, which resulted in further FTA negotiations in the region. In 2003, the US-Singapore FTA was signed. The USA also expressed its interests in negotiating a trade agreement with Thailand to strengthen trade ties with countries in the region that are actively pursuing economic reforms. During several rounds of FTA negotiations between both countries in the subsequent years, good progress was made on the content of the agreement; however, it has not been signed yet.

A dynamic increase in the number of bilateral and multilateral FTAs in East Asia in the 21st century has preliminarily concerned such countries as China, India, Singapore and South Korea, which can nowadays boast of over 40 trade agreements of different status (proposed, negotiated, signed or discontinued) with partners inside and outside the region. Nowadays the total number of such FTAs in the Asia Pacific is estimated at 810 (Table 3.2).

Table 3.2 FTAs according to their status in the region of East Asia and the Asia Pacific, 2022

Country	*Proposed/under consultation and study*	*Negotiations launched*	*Signed but not yet in effect*	*Signed and in effect*	*Discontinued*	*Total*
Australia	5	4	2	17	2[a]	30
Brunei	8	1	0	11	1[b]	21
Cambodia	6	1	1	9	0	17
China	15	9	2	21	0	47
Hong Kong	1	1	0	8	0	10
India	12	16	0	15	0	44
Indonesia	17	6	3	15	0	41
Japan	7	6	0	20	1[b]	34
Laos	5	1	0	10	0	16
Malaysia	9	6	1	17	1	35
Myanmar	5	2	0	8	0	16
New Zealand	5	6	1	13	1[b]	26
Philippines	14	3	0	10	0	27
Singapore	6	7	1	27	3[c]	44
South Korea	10	10	3	19	0	42
Taiwan	5	1	0	8	0	14
Thailand	14	9	0	15	0	39
Vietnam	8	3	0	15	1[b]	27

Source: Own elaboration based on the Asia Regional Integration Center (2022).

[a] The Australia-United Arab Emirates Free Trade Agreement (Australia-UAE FTA) (now Australia-GCC FTA) was discontinued in 2005 and the TPP – in March 2018.

[b] The discontinued agreement is TPP.

[c] The Singapore-Bahrain Free Trade Agreement (Singapore-Bahrain FTA) was discontinued in August 2013, the Singapore-Jordan Free Trade Agreement (SJFTA) – in September 2013, and the third discontinued agreement is the TPP.

Singapore is currently characterised by the greatest number of FTAs signed and in effect – 27, followed by China (21), Japan (20) and South Korea (19). The mentioned countries were first engaged in lengthy negotiations; then, they have become members of a mega-regional agreement, the RCEP. All of them have concluded FTAs with the USA. Singapore and South Korea signed bilateral FTAs with the USA in 2004 and 2012, respectively. Japan first concluded an agreement with the USA in frames of a mega-regional agreement, the Trans-Pacific Partnership (TPP), but eventually the USA withdrew from it. In 2020, both countries signed the Japan-US FTA. Also, in 2020, China concluded an economic and trade agreement with the USA – in a form of the Economic and Trade Agreement between the Government of the United States of America and the Government of People's Republic of China (PRC-US Economic and Trade Agreement).

Additionally, South Korea, Japan and Singapore have concluded FTAs with the EU. In 2011, the Republic of Korea-European Union Free Trade Agreement (Republic of Korea-EU FTA) entered into force, then in 2019 – the Japan-European Union Economic Partnership Agreement (Japan-EU EPA) and the Singapore-European Union Free Trade Agreement (Singapore-EU FTA). An FTA between China and the EU was proposed in 2014, but it has not been concluded yet. Also, in 2020, Vietnam and the EU signed a bilateral FTA, and in 2021, the Indonesia-European Union Comprehensive Economic Partnership Agreement (Indonesia-EU CEPA) entered into force. Trade co-operation was also formally established with other European countries in a form of bilateral FTAs with Island (PRC-Island FTA, 2014), Switzerland (Japan-Switzerland, 2009; PRC-Switzerland FTA, 2014), Turkey (Republic of Korea-Turkey FTA, 2013; Malaysia-Turkey FTA, 2015; Singapore-Turkey FTA, 2017) and more recently, with the UK (Japan-United Kingdom FTA, 2021; Singapore-United Kingdom FTA, 2021; United Kingdom-Vietnam FTA, 2021; Republic of Korea-United Kingdom FTA, 2022). Additionally, there have been negotiated FTAs between China and Norway (since 2009) and China and Moldova (since 2017), as well as the bilateral Economic Partnership Agreement between South Korea and Russia (since 2019).

At the level of the region of East Asia, China successfully signed and implemented bilateral FTAs with Thailand (October 2003), Singapore (January 2009), South Korea (December 2015) and recently with Cambodia (January 2022). Since March 2013, Japan, South Korea and China have been launching a tripartite agreement, Japan-Republic of Korea-People's Republic of China Free Trade Agreement (Japan-Republic of Korea-PRC FTA), which can be perceived as an effective measure to mitigate the disproportion in the mutual trade relations in the region of Northeast Asia as a result of entering into force the PRC-Republic of Korea FTA. Additionally, China signed economic and trade agreements, so called Closer Economic Partnership Agreements, with its separate customs territories – Macao and Hong Kong in 2019 and 2020, respectively. In turn, in 2010, China and Taiwan signed the Economic Cooperation Framework Agreement aiming at reducing tariffs and commercial barriers between two sides (Table 3.3).

Whereas the dynamic increase of bilateral (and multilateral) FTAs was observed in the first decade of the 21st century in Asia, the second decade of the third millennium is determined by a new generation of region-wide FTAs – mega-FTAs,[1] like the RCEP and the CPTPP, which have accelerated regional integration in East Asia and the Asia Pacific. The emergence of mega-FTAs in Asia is believed not to be a random phenomenon, but it is connected to the evolution of institutionalised economic integration in the region. Contemporarily two competing pathways of East Asian integration can be distinguished – the East Asian direction in the format of regional FTAs and the trans-Pacific orientation. The former embraces, e.g., ASEAN and AEC, as the realisation of Southeast Asia's end goal of economic integration as well as

Table 3.3 FTAs concluded by individual East Asian countries within the region, 2022

Country	*Brunei*	*Cambodia*	*China*	*Hong Kong*	*Indonesia*	*Japan*	*Lao*	*Malaysia*	*Myanmar*	*Philippines*	*Singapore*	*South Korea*	*Taiwan*	*Thailand*	*Vietnam*	*ASEAN*
Brunei						S/E										
Cambodia			S/E									S/NE				
China		S/E		S/E		N					S/E	S/E	S/E	S/E		S/E
Hong Kong			S/E										P			S/E
Indonesia						S/E						S/NE	P			
Japan	S/E		N		S/E			S/E		S/E	S/E	N		S/E	S/E	S/E
Lao														S/E		
Malaysia						S/E						N				
Myanmar						S/E										
Philippines						S/E						N	P			
Singapore			S/E			S/E						S/E	S/E			
South Korea		S/NE	S/E		S/NE	N		N		N	S/E			P	S/E	S/E
Taiwan			S/E	P	P					P	S/E					
Thailand			S/E			S/E	S/E					P				
Vietnam						S/E						S/E				
ASEAN			S/E	S/E		S/E						S/E				

Source: Own elaboration based on Asia Regional Integration Center (2022).

Abbreviations: P, proposed/under consultation and study; N, negotiations launched; S/NE, signed but not yet in effect; S/E, signed and in effect.

East Asia Free Trade Agreement (EAFTA/ASEAN+3 FTA), Comprehensive Economic Partnership for East Asia (CEPEA/ASEAN+6 FTA) and RCEP, whereas the latter covers, e.g., Trans-Pacific Strategic Economic Partnership Agreement and CPTPP and their potential consolidation into a Free Trade Area of the Asia-Pacific (FTAAP).

The withdrawal of the USA from TPP as well as not considering it in RCEP explicitly indicates the East Asian direction in the institutionalisation of economic integration and the increasing strategic position of China in the region. However, despite the fact that the USA has not become a party of neither of the mega-FTAs in the region (CPTPP and RCEP), it has been paying a substantial role in determining the directions of cooperation in both East Asia and the Asia Pacific. The USA has been actively engaged in deepening the trans-Pacific institutional integration, for example by participating in regional cooperation under the auspices of APEC, supporting the creation of institutions in East Asia as well as the involvement in other East Asian institutional structures, like the East Asia Summit (EAS). The example of the direction of regional cooperation with the US leading role is currently the Free and Open Indo-Pacific (FOIP), which are the Indo-Pacific-specific strategies of countries with similar interests in the region.

While analysing the directions of East Asia's economic integration, it is also worth mentioning the FTAAP, which represents an aspiration among the 21-member economies of APEC but is currently not under negotiation. Within APEC, the aspiration to establish free and open trade and investment in the Asia Pacific by 2020 was first outlined in the Bogor Goals of 1994, and then specified by APEC's leaders in the Lima Declaration on FTAAP in 2016. The Declaration assumes that FTAAP will be realised "outside of APEC, parallel with the APEC process", built upon "ongoing undertakings, and through possible pathways, including the Trans-Pacific Partnership (TPP) and Regional Comprehensive Economic Partnership (RCEP)" (APEC, 2016). Table 3.4 presents the summary of signed, negotiated and proposed regional and region-wide (trans-regional and mega-regional) trade agreements in East Asia and the Asia Pacific, concluded with the participation of East Asian countries.

In consideration of the above, it can be concluded that despite its institutional deficiency in a formal sense, East Asia's economic integration, characterised by its market-driven and informal nature, has been impressive in a practical sense, as indicated by the great number of bilateral FTAs concluded in the region. This informal, "network-style" integration could even be perceived as a feasible substitute for formal institutionalisation of economic relations in the region. However, over the past years, the traditional institutional equilibrium of East Asia's economic integration – the embrace of the WTO at the multilateral level – and the concentration on informal, market-driven economic integration in the regional dimension have evolved towards the pursuit of greater institutionalisation at the multilateral level in the regional and global dimension. It is exemplified by an increased number of FTAs concluded with countries both within and outside the region, constituting a great web of regional trade arrangements (RTAs). However, the East Asian commitment to a broader, multilateral trade regime has, partially, turned impractical considering duplicating, overlapping and sometimes even excluding mechanisms and institutions, causing the "spaghetti bowl effect" or in the Asian reality, the "noodle bowl" effect, which sometimes instead of facilitating economic integration even more complicates it. Since the second decade of the 21st century, a new wave of regionalism in East Asia, marked by the emergence of two mega-FTAs (CPTPP and RCEP), can be observed – and the question remains whether they will mitigate or accentuate the "noodle bowl effect" in the region?

In literature the opinions on the potential impact of both CPTPP and RCEP on East Asian trade framework are shared. Syadullah and Ardiansyah (2017) argued that the unification of the 16 countries in RCEP may be expected to reduce the spaghetti bowl effect caused by a number of FTAs. However, because RCEP does not eliminate the existing FTAs in the region, it tends to add to a new chain of new spaghetti. Park (2022) noticed that the increasingly competitive formation of bilateral FTAs and hub-and-spoke plurilateral FTAs has produced a complicated web of overlapping FTAs in East Asia; hence,

Table 3.4 Regional and region-wide FTAs in East Asia and the Asia Pacific, 1976–2022

Name of the agreement	*Member states*	*Status*
Asia-Pacific Trade Agreement	Bangladesh, China, India, Laos, Sri Lanka, South Korea	Signed and in effect (1976)
ASEAN Free Trade Area (AFTA)	ASEAN	Signed and in effect (1993)
Shanghai Cooperation Organisation Free Trade Agreement (SCO FTA)	China, Kazakhstan, Kyrgyzstan, Russia, Tajikistan, Uzbekistan	Proposed (2003)
East Asia Free Trade Area (EAFTA)	ASEAN+3	Proposed (2004)
ASEAN+	ASEAN-China Comprehensive Economic Cooperation Agreement	Signed and in effect (2005)
	ASEAN-Republic of Korea Comprehensive Economic Cooperation Agreement	Signed and in effect (2007)
	ASEAN-Japan Comprehensive Economic Partnership	Signed and in effect (2008)
	ASEAN-Australia, New Zealand Free Trade Agreement	Signed and in effect (2010)
	ASEAN-India Comprehensive Economic Cooperation Agreement	Signed and in effect (2010)
	ASEAN-Hong Kong Free Trade Agreement	Signed and in effect (2019)
	ASEAN-EU Free Trade Agreement	Proposed (2007)
	ASEAN-Pakistan Free Trade Agreement	Proposed (2009)
	ASEAN-Eurasian Economic Union Free Trade Agreement	Proposed (2016)
	ASEAN-Canada Free Trade Agreement	Negotiations launched (2021)
Comprehensive Economic Partnership for East Asia (CEPEA/ASEAN+6)	ASEAN+6 = ASEAN+3 + India, Australia and New Zealand	Proposed (2005)
Trans-Pacific Strategic Economic Partnership Agreement (Trans-Pacific SEP)	Brunei, Chile, New Zealand, Singapore	Signed and in effect (2006)
Preferential Tariff Arrangement Group of Eight Developing Countries (D-8)	Bangladesh, Egypt, Indonesia, Iran, Malaysia, Nigeria, Pakistan, Turkey	Signed and in effect (2011)

(*Continued*)

Table 3.4 (Continued)

Name of the agreement	*Member states*	*Status*
Free Trade Area of the Asia Pacific (FTAAP)	Australia, Brunei, Canada, Chile, China, Hong Kong, Russia, Indonesia, Japan, Malaysia, Mexico, New Zealand, Papua New Guinea, Peru, Philippines, Singapore, South Korea, Taiwan, Thailand, USA, Vietnam	Proposed (2014)
Trade Preferential System of the Organisation of the Islamic Conference (TPS-OIC)	Bahrain, Bangladesh, Benin, Burkina Faso, Cameroon, Chad, Comoros, Cote Divoire, Djibouti, Egypt, Gabon, Gambia, Guinea, Guinea-Bissau Indonesia, Iran, Iraq, Jordan, Kuwait, Lebanon, Libya, Malaysia, Maldives, Mauritania, Morocco, Niger, Nigeria, Oman, Pakistan, Palestine, Qatar, Saudi Arabia, Senegal, Sierra Leone, Somalia, Sudan, Syria, Tunisia, Turkey, UAE, Uganda	Signed but not yet in effect (2014)
Bay of Bengal Initiative for Multi-Sectoral Technical and Economic Cooperation (BIMSTEC) Free Trade Area	Bangladesh, Bhutan, India, Myanmar, Nepal, Sri Lanka, Thailand	Negotiated (2014)
Australia-New Zealand Pacific Alliance (FTA)	Australia, Chile, Colombia, Mexico, New Zealand, Peru	Negotiated (2017)
Trans-Pacific Partnership (TPP)	Australia, Brunei, Chile, Japan, Canada, Malaysia, New Zealand, Peru, Singapore, Vietnam, USA	Discontinued (2018) Signed but not yet in effect in 2016
Comprehensive and Progressive Agreement for Trans-Pacific Partnership (CPTPP)	Australia, Brunei, Chile, Japan, Canada, Malaysia, New Zealand, Peru, Singapore, Vietnam	Signed and in effect (2018)
Republic of Korea-Pacific Alliance Free Trade Agreement	South Korea, Chile, Colombia, Mexico, Peru	Proposed (2018)
Regional Comprehensive Economic Partnership in East Asia (RCEP)	ASEAN+3 + Australia and New Zealand	Signed and in effect (2022)

Source: Own elaboration based on the Asia Regional Integration Center (2022).

considering the potentially harmful "spaghetti-bowl effect" of overlapping RTAs and deepening intra-regional production networks, a few "mega-lateral" RTAs have been negotiated, including CPTPP and RCEP.

In turn, Dieter (2020, 2021) remarked that RCEP ends the opacity of trade agreements in the Asia-Pacific. For companies, the reduction of tariffs in bilateral trade resulted in increased administrative costs. Companies had to spend a lot of money to document the origin of a product. Without a valid certificate of origin, a product does not qualify for any benefits or tariff exemptions in any free-trade arrangement. RCEP has contributed to limiting the administrative burden on trading companies. Owing to its implementation, there will be a single set of rules of origin for all participating economies.

It is also argued that RCEP provides a means to simplify the processes and procedures for each FTA (RCEP-member countries have currently existing trade agreements with associated FTA partners) and reduce any existing trade inefficiencies, eventually, avoiding the "spaghetti/noodle bowl" effect, where ASEAN could become entangled with multiple FTAs with different rules and tariff rates for each country. As such, according to Spire Research and Consulting (2024), RCEP can serve as a building block foundation for the multilateral trading system. Businesses will only need to follow one set of procedures rather than navigate several different sets of trading rules with RCEP partners.

Minghui (2017) remarked that RCEP intends to create an open market with a higher degree of liberalisation than the five "ASEAN +1" FTAs and it aims to integrate East Asia's complex FTA networks and to remedy the "noodle bowl effect" of FTA proliferation in the region. These complex FTA arrangements complicate rules of origin and include red tape and cross-border procedures that increase transaction costs, reduce enterprises' operational efficiency and ignite trade protectionism, producing a negative impact on East Asian production networks. Also, Intan (2020) claimed that much of the economic gains from RCEP will come from mitigating the Asian "noodle bowl" effect. According to the scholar, the agreement will harmonise what have to date been separate rules of origin across the region into several cumulative schemes, with the changes allowing advanced manufacturing supply chains.

The author of this book agrees that, potentially, a large number of RTAs in force may unintentionally result in a "spaghetti/noodle bowl" effect – where each different country partnership requires a different set of trade rules and processes, resulting in trade inefficiencies and deterring businesses. It is also true that CPTPP as well as RCEP members are simultaneously parties to several overlapping RTAs, and RCEP is another trade agreement, besides CPTPP, in the region, partially embracing the CPTPP countries and to some extent duplicating the CPTPP's text. Nevertheless, the author also thinks that developing a multilateral agreement, like CPTPP or RCEP, could mitigate the issue of the Asian "noodle bowl effect" and ideally supersede all the different bilateral partnerships and develop common rules, such as the rules of origin.

Note

1 Mega-FTAs are deep integration partnerships in the form of FTAs between countries or regions with a major share of world trade and FDI, in which two or more of the parties serve as hubs in global value chains (GVCs). Therefore, it is predicted that mega-FTAs would establish global trade governance over the most dynamic element of the world trade – the supply chain trade, which the current WTO rules could not properly regulate and support (Baldwin, 2012).

4 East Asia's institutionalised regionalism of the 21st century and implications for Europe

With the evolution of the institutionalisation of East Asia's economic integration, several institutional complexes have been established in the region, like, e.g., Association of Southeast Asian Nations (ASEAN), ASEAN Economic Community, ASEAN Plus Three and East Asia Summit in East Asia as well as Asia Pacific Economic Cooperation (APEC), Comprehensive and Progressive Agreement for Trans-Pacific Partnership (CPTPP) and Regional Comprehensive Economic Partnership (RCEP) in the Asia-Pacific region. Moreover, there are numerous regional free trade agreement (FTAs) of a bilateral and multilateral character that have been discussed in the previous chapter. This chapter analyses East Asia's institutionalised regionalism of the 21st through the prism of the newly concluded trade agreements, CPTPP and RCEP, providing a comparative analysis of the aforementioned institutions, including their antecedents and evolution as well as attributes reflected in different levels of liberalisation. The considerations are complemented with the presentation of actual and potential economic effects in terms of GDP and trade flows of both CPTPP and RCEP and their implications for Europe and the European Union (EU).

4.1 Comprehensive and Progressive Agreement for Trans-Pacific Partnership

The CPTPP is a comprehensive FTA formed by the 11 remaining members of the proposed Trans-Pacific Partnership (TPP) after US withdrawal in 2017. CPTPP is in effect for all parties – entering into force for Australia, Canada, Japan, Mexico, New Zealand and Singapore in 2018; Vietnam in 2019; Peru in 2021; Malaysia and Chile in 2022 and Brunei in 2023. To date the UK, China, Taiwan, Ecuador, Costa Rica, Uruguay and Ukraine have formally applied to join CPTPP. The UK is to become the first new member, after reaching the agreement in 2023 on accession terms.

4.1.1 Origins and the establishment of CPTPP

The origins of the CPTPP (or TPP-11) trace back to the TPP – a proposed trade agreement between 12 Pacific Rim economies: Australia, Brunei, Canada, Chile,

DOI: 10.4324/9781003544234-4

Japan, Malaysia, Mexico, New Zealand, Peru, Singapore, the USA and Vietnam. The proposal was signed in 2016 but not ratified. In turn, the predecessor of TPP was the Trans-Pacific Strategic Economic Partnership (or P4), which was signed by four Pacific Rim countries – Brunei, Chile, New Zealand and Singapore in 2005 – with the intention, among others, to reduce and eliminate trade tariffs between the member countries.

Additionally, Brunei, Chile, New Zealand and Singapore were involved in the negotiations for the TPP, together with other eight countries – Australia, Canada, Japan, Malaysia, Mexico, Peru, the USA and Vietnam. In 2017, Japan, as the first country, ratified TPP, followed by New Zealand. However, in the same year, the Trump Administration withdrew the USA as a signatory of TPP and from TPP negotiations. Interestingly, simultaneously, Japan officially completed the domestic procedure for the ratification of TPP. Because of the US withdrawal from TPP, the provisions of the agreement could not be legally binding pursuant to Art. 30.5.2, as the necessary condition for entering into force was the ratification by at least six of the original signatories, together representing at least 85% of the combined GDP of the original signatories in 2013. Considering the fact that the two largest TPP members – the USA and Japan – accounted for 80% of the TPP countries' GDP, the US withdrawal scuttled the chances for implementing the agreement in the initial form.

Nevertheless, the prime ministers of the other 11 countries, led by Japan, agreed on the final implementation of the agreement despite the withdrawal of the US party. Consequently, in 2018, they signed the CPTPP Agreement, which largely transposes from the original TPP Agreement provisions.

4.1.2 CPTPP commitments

The CPTPP is a comprehensive FTA, committed to support sustainable and inclusive economic development. As stated in the Preamble, the parties of the Agreement resolve to "establish comprehensive regional agreement that promotes economic integration to liberalise trade and investment, bring economic growth and social benefits, create new opportunities for workers and businesses, contribute to raising living standards, benefit consumers, reduce poverty and promote sustainable growth".[1]

CPTPP incorporates 30 original chapters of the original TPP text, such as: (1) initial provisions and general definitions; (2) national treatment and access to the goods market; (3) rules of origin (RoOs); (4) textile and apparel goods; (5) customs administration and trade facilitation; (6) trade remedies; (7) sanitary and phytosanitary measures; (8) technical barriers to trade; (9) investment; (10) trade in services; (11) financial services; (12) temporary movement of business persons; (13) telecommunications; (14) electronic commerce; (15) government procurement; (16) competition policy; (17) state-owned enterprises (SOEs) and designated monopolies; (18) intellectual property; (19) labour; (20) environment; (21) cooperation and competence development; (22)

competitiveness and business facilitation; (23) development; (24) small- and medium-sized enterprises (SMEs); (25) regulatory coherence; (26) transparency and anti-corruption; (27) administrative and institutional provisions; (28) dispute settlement (DS); (29) exceptions and general provisions and (30) final provisions. However, CPTPP suspends indefinitely 22 TPP-specific commitments, which had been US priorities and which CPTPP members may reinstate through consensus. CPTPP also establishes new administrative procedures (e.g., accession) that replace those in TPP. Key CPTPP provisions include:

- Goods Tariffs. Immediate elimination of most tariffs among current members and eventual elimination of tariffs on roughly 99% of tariff lines. Tariff commitments for new members are subject to accession negotiations.
- E-Commerce/Digital Trade. Requires free cross-border data flows and prohibits requirements to localise computing facilities, with certain public policy exceptions. Prohibits duties on digital products and requirements to share source code to gain market entry. Requires members to have privacy regimes in place nationally.
- Environment. Requires countries to enforce and not derogate from their environmental laws to attract trade and investment, implement specified multilateral environmental agreements they have joined, prohibit certain fishing subsidies and combat illegal wildlife trade. *A provision broadening illegal wildlife trade to include determinations based on a trade partner's laws was suspended.*
- Government Procurement. Requires non-discriminatory treatment towards domestic and foreign firms in government purchasing decisions above certain thresholds. *Two suspended provisions relate to: procuring entities and efforts to promote compliance with labour laws and a mandate to reopen procurement negotiations in three years.*
- Intellectual Property Rights (IPRs). Protects patents, copyrights and trademarks, and includes disciplines on trade secrets to combat cyber-theft, with various phase-in periods, notably for Vietnam. *Protections were narrowed due to suspensions relating to: scope of patentability, patent term extensions, test data for marketing approvals and requirements for criminal penalties for certain IP infringements. Also suspended are: biologics commitments, extended term for copyrights, and provisions on legal remedies and safe harbour for internet service providers.*
- Investment. Removes barriers and provides protections for foreign investors in CPTPP countries, including non-discriminatory and minimum standards of treatment, though each country has exempted some sectors or practices. Includes investor-state dispute settlement (ISDS), though countries may block investors' claims against tobacco control measures. *Due to suspensions, ISDS does not apply to certain disputes such as investment agreements between investors and a central government authority (e.g., relating to natural resource rights or infrastructure).*

- RoOs. Sets requirements to determine whether goods originate within the territory of CPTPP members and are eligible for CPTPP benefits (e.g., cars require 45%–55% regional value content depending on calculation method to qualify for tariff elimination).
- Services. Provides core obligations of non-discrimination (national treatment and most-favoured nation [MFN] treatment), market access and local presence on a "negative list" basis (i.e., covering all cross-border services sectors, except those specifically excluded). Includes separate obligations for financial services, with sector-specific exemptions.
- SOEs. Requires countries to direct SOEs to make purchase and sale decisions based on commercial considerations, enforce regulations with regard to SOEs impartially and ensure subsidies and other non-commercial assistance to SOEs do not cause harm to other member countries, with exceptions, including for smaller (revenue) SOEs and provision of public services.
- Worker Rights. Requires countries to adopt and not derogate from laws consistent with core International Labour Organization principles and rights on freedom of association and collective bargaining, and elimination of forced labour, child labour and employment discrimination in matters related to trade and investment. *US-proposed bilateral labour plans with Brunei, Malaysia and Vietnam, which included additional commitments (e.g., allowing for independent unions in Vietnam), are excluded from CPTPP.*
- DS. Includes a DS mechanism to enforce commitments, though some exemptions apply.
- Accession. Requires unanimous consent among members to begin market access negotiations (the UK has been the only applicant to reach this step). If talks proceed, then parties are to determine whether an applicant is qualified to join based on market access offers (e.g., tariffs) and ability to adhere to CPTPP rules. Such approval for China may be difficult for, given global concerns about its trade practices and industrial policies.

4.1.3 Trade liberalisation under CPTPP

Already in the original TPP, tariffs remained a problem for supply chains because even small tariff rates can be deeply damaging to complex products, as the total size of embedded tariffs in items that repeatedly cross borders can be substantial. Hence, TPP needed to cut all tariffs to zero to facilitate trade among member states. The CPTPP Agreement incorporates the tariff outcomes contained in the original TPP text. The elimination of customs duties is implemented progressively over time on the basis of each party's Annex 2-D schedules of tariff commitments (Article 2.4). Once fully implemented, 99% of tariff lines among the CPTPP parties will be duty-free. Most tariff lines became duty-free when the Agreement entered into force for each CPTPP country. Tariffs on other goods will be eliminated gradually over "phase-out" periods, which vary by country and are detailed in each country's respective tariff elimination schedules. Within CPTPP, Singapore was the fastest to implement concessions – all at entry into force – while the longest transition period of 21 years applies in the case of imports by Japan and Vietnam. Tariffs are reduced from the base rate specified in the parties' schedules, drawn up on the basis of the Harmonised System (HS) 2012. Under CPTPP, the "base rate" is the tariff, which was applied on 1st January 2010 and used as the base for negotiations. Irrespective of CPTPP, each CPTPP member is also able to unilaterally reduce its tariff at any time, which could mean that a particular country may apply a lower MFN tariff rate than the current rate set out in the CPTPP Tariff Elimination Schedule (e.g., a country might temporarily reduce a tariff for a commodity that is in short supply). Overall, the trading parties can assess whether it is more advantageous to import under the preferential CPTPP tariff under the Agreement, under the current MFN applied tariff or through a separate FTA.

Under the CPTPP Agreement, the first six countries ratifying the Agreement, i.e., Australia, Canada, Japan, Mexico, New Zealand and Singapore, have the right to notify to the later ratifying countries about the schedule of tariff concessions. The first tariff cut for the initial six countries to ratify CPTPP took place on 30th December 2018. The second tariff cut for each of the initial six countries, except Japan, took place on 1st January 2019. Japan's second tariff cut took place on 1st April 2019. CPTPP also provides for a catch-up mechanism for "late-comers" – i.e., implementing at once all tariff cuts already in force for other parties. Thus, although CPTPP entered into force for Vietnam and Peru later than for Australia, Canada, Japan, Mexico, New Zealand and Singapore, Vietnam's and Peru's tariff schedules should be read as if the Agreement entered into force for them on 30th December 2018. For practical purposes, this means that each country's tariff schedule should be read as if its first tariff cut took effect on 30th December 2018, with subsequent tariff cuts taking effect on 1st January each year (except for Japan, in which case each tariff cut takes effect on 1st April each year).

At the entry into force of CPTPP, between 31.4% and 72.3% of the parties' MFN applied tariffs were duty-free, whereas in the case of Singapore – 99.9%. As the Agreement was entering into force, Australia, Canada, Mexico and New Zealand liberalised their tariff lines. Singapore liberalised almost all lines immediately. At the end of implementation, only New Zealand and Singapore will remove tariffs on all lines for their partners. The lowest liberalisation will be that by Japan – 95.9% of tariff lines by the end of implementation – while for others more than 98% of tariff lines will be liberalised. Table 4.1 summarises liberalisation under the CPTPP Agreement for Australia, Canada, Japan, Mexico, New Zealand, Singapore and Vietnam in terms of the percentage of lines becoming duty-free at entry into force and during the implementation period, as well as provides information on the percentage of lines that were

Table 4.1 Liberalisation of tariff lines under CPTPP

Party	*MFN duty-free at entry into force*	*Liberalisation under CPTPP, % of lines*		*Remain dutiable*
		At entry into force	*During implementation period*	
Australia	47.7	45.6	6.5	0.2
Canada	72.3	21.7	4.6	1.3
Japan	40.3	43.9–44.0	11.6–11.8	4.1
Mexico	57.2	18.1–18.3	23.9	0.6–0.8
New Zealand	59.1	35.5	5.4	–
Singapore	99.9	0.1	–	–
Vietnam	31.4	35.4	31.5	1.7

Source: Own elaboration based on WTO (2021).

CPTPP, Comprehensive and Progressive Agreement for Trans-Pacific Partnership; MFN, most-favoured nation.

MFN duty-free at entry into force as well as those remaining dutiable following the CPTPP's full implementation.

Summing up, several defining attributes make CPTPP an important agreement of the 21st century, setting a new standard for world trade. One of the characteristics is providing comprehensive market access, by eliminating or reducing tariff and non-tariff barriers across substantially all trade in goods and services and covering the full spectrum of trade, including goods and services, trade and investment. Secondly, CPTPP ensures the regional approach to commitments, such as developing production and supply chains, enhancing efficiency, supporting and creating jobs, raising living standards, enhancing conservation efforts, facilitating cross-border integration and reciprocally opening domestic markets. Also, it addresses new trade challenges, including the development of the digital economy and the role of SOEs in the world economy. Last but not least, TPP provides the opportunity for economies of different levels of development, and enterprises of different sizes can benefit from international trade, constituting a platform for regional economic integration across the Asia-Pacific region. However, it is worth highlighting that although CPTPP retains the major attributes of the original TPP, it lacks the essential feature related to the presence of a strong core in the form of a bilateral agreement between the USA and Japan. In comparison to the original TPP, CPTPP is an agreement with a lower potential to have a significant impact on the regional trade and investment architecture. Thus, CPTPP may not constitute a strong alternative to integration processes and initiatives undertaken in East Asia, which are highly affected by the growing geopolitical position of China as well as the mega-regional trade framework of the RCEP.

4.2 Regional Comprehensive Economic Partnership

The RCEP is a comprehensive FTA among the Asia-Pacific countries of Australia, Brunei, Cambodia, China, Indonesia, Japan, South Korea, Laos, Malaysia, Myanmar, New Zealand, the Philippines, Singapore, Thailand and Vietnam. The RCEP Agreement was signed on 15th November 2020, entering into force on 1st January 2022 for the first ten ratifying countries (Australia, Brunei, Cambodia, China, Japan, Laos, New Zealand, Singapore, Thailand and Vietnam) and on 1st February 2022 for South Korea. As for the remaining signatories, the Agreement entered into force 60 days after the deposit of their respective instrument of ratification, acceptance or approval to the Secretary-General of ASEAN as the Depository of the RCEP Agreement. Any other country or separate customs territory in the region can accede to the Agreement from 1st July 2023 onwards. Bangladesh, Hong Kong, Sri Lanka and Chile have formally applied for membership in RCEP, whereas the UK considers their potential involvement in the Agreement.

4.2.1 RCEP history

After the Asian financial crisis of 1997–1998, East Asian countries turned from APEC to the ASEAN+3 cooperation and engaged in the creation of vaguely defined East Asian Community. Initially, regional economic integration in East Asia had a character of a bilateral rather than regional cooperation among ASEAN and Northeast Asian countries. Nevertheless, the establishment of a region-wide FTA was considered, firstly only in the form of the East Asia Free Trade Area (EAFTA) with ASEAN+3 countries, and subsequently in the form of the Comprehensive Economic Partnership for East Asia (CEPEA), comprising ASEAN+6 members. Whereas EAFTA was supported by China, CEPEA was promoted by Japan, which aimed at counterbalancing China's increasing regional influence by inviting Australia, New Zealand and India for the participation in the East Asian regional framework (Urata, 2009). It is worth emphasising here that Australia was always considered as a reliable partner for Japan in regional cooperation. In turn, India was taken in account as a member of the East Asian integration grouping as a promising destination for Japanese companies, where they could extend their regional production networks. Both countries were also targeted by Japan to strengthen its security and economic relations with other countries than the USA.

After several years of exploring EAFTA and CEPEA, in 2011, ASEAN countries initiated the creation of RCEP (or ASEAN+6). One of the most important reasons for launching RCEP negotiations in 2012 was to consolidate all existing ASEAN+1 FTAs into one trade agreement due to the fact that they envisaged different levels of liberalisation and most of them lacked important trade and trade-related commitments (e.g., digital trade, IPRs). Moreover, ASEAN strived to retain its central position and leading role in regional economic integration at a time when trilateral cooperation among Japan, China and South Korea was tightened during the global economic crisis. Eventually, China also supported the establishment of an ASEAN+6 FTA in the form of RCEP. The change of China's approach towards the creation of a region-wide FTA was highly influenced by the strategic pivot to Asia, new Asia-Pacific strategy of the USA, which assumed the establishment of the TPP. Additionally, Japan's intention to participate in TPP negotiations had a significant impact on China's decision to join RCEP.

RCEP negotiations, which were launched in 2012, originally included 16 countries – Australia, Brunei, Cambodia, China, India, Indonesia, Japan, Laos, Malaysia, Myanmar, New Zealand, the Philippines, Singapore, South Korea, Thailand and Vietnam. India, which took part in the initial negotiations but in 2019 decided to opt out, was invited to join RCEP at any time. Some experts argue that India's politicians were concerned about liberalisation on politically important industries in the manufacturing sector and in agriculture as well as long-standing commitment to self-sufficiency. Others seek the reasons of India's withdrawal, preliminarily, in concerns about an influx of Chinese products, lack of liberalisation in services sectors and geopolitical dynamics with China.

4.2.2 Scope and objectives of RCEP

The RCEP Agreement comprises 20 chapters; the first chapter (1) is dedicated to initial provisions and general definitions, and subsequent chapters cover such issues as: trade in goods (2), RoOs (3), customs procedures and trade facilitation (4), sanitary and phytosanitary measures (5), standards, technical regulations and conformity assessment procedures (6), trade remedies (7), trade in services (8), temporary movement of natural persons (9), investment (10), IPRs (11), electronic commerce (12), competition (13), SMEs (14), economic and technical cooperation (15), government procurement (16), general provisions and exceptions (17), institutional provisions (18) as well as DS (19). The last chapter (20) relates to the final provisions of the Agreement. Several provisions, e.g., related to investment protection and e-commerce, are new to ASEAN FTAs. The RCEP Agreement is considered a "living agreement", with a built-in agenda for further talks in various areas.

The scope and objectives of RCEP, as well as of previously mentioned CPTPP, have considerably been determined by the member counties' development (income) level, but also by whom the mega-FTA was initiated – the ASEAN or the USA. The general objectives of RCEP are outlined in Chapter 1, Article 1 of the RCEP Agreement. Firstly, RCEP aims at establishing a modern, comprehensive, high quality and mutually beneficial economic partnership framework to facilitate trade and investment and contribute to global economic growth. Secondly, it focuses on the liberalisation of trade in goods by progressive elimination of tariff and non-tariff barriers as well as the liberalisation of trade in services by eliminating restrictions and discriminatory measures. Thirdly, RCEP aims to create liberal, facilitative, and competitive investment environment in the region. Key commitments of the RCEP Agreement are as following:

- Tariff schedule. Reduces or eliminates tariffs by approximately 92% over 20 years, with eliminated tariffs/quotas covering over 65% of goods traded. There are sizable carveouts in certain sectors, such as agriculture in the case of Japan. Due to existing FTAs, tariff reductions are not necessarily substantial for all of the parties.
- Services. While seven members agreed to a "negative list" approach that restricts only those sectors listed explicitly, eight members (including China) negotiated to keep a "positive list" approach that only liberalises the sectors they list in the agreement – these countries committed to transition to a negative list within six years. Some estimates suggest that at least 65% of services sectors will be fully open, with advanced market access in professional, financial, telecommunications, computer and logistics services.
- Investment protections. Prohibit more extensive performance requirements than previous commitments (e.g., technology transfer as a condition of market access). RCEP does not include ISDS, though parties commit to review its inclusion within five years.
- E-commerce. Requires not to impose customs duties on electronic transmissions. General obligations to prevent data localisation requirements or cross-border data transfers are subjected to broad exceptions for national security and public policy reasons. The e-commerce chapter, like some others, is not subjected to general DS.
- Special and differential treatment. RCEP parties, particularly least developed countries (Burma, Cambodia, Laos), and ASEAN members negotiated "special and differential treatment" that largely offers transitional periods for various commitments (e.g., related to e-commerce, trade facilitation and IPRs).

4.2.3 Trade liberalisation under RCEP

RCEP economies are generally open to trade, both because of their pretty low World Trade Organisation (WTO) MFN rates and because of their participation in the regional trade agreements, which results in relatively low tariffs for intra-RCEP trade overall. Nevertheless, there are some substantial differences across the RCEP members. Table 4.2 presents average effectively applied tariffs on intra-RCEP trade, excluding concessions. For example, Australia, Brunei, New Zealand and Singapore have liberalised all or almost all trade originating from other RCEP countries, whereas overall tariffs on imports from the RCEP countries are relatively higher for South Korea (4.8%),

Table 4.2 Average tariffs on intra-RCEP trade (excluding concessions)

Country	*Overall*	*Agriculture*	*Natural resources*	*Manufacturing*
Australia	0.0	0.0	0.0	0.0
Brunei	0.0	0.0	0.0	0.0
Cambodia	3.3	0.6	0.0	4.0
China	2.8	6.7	0.4	3.1
Indonesia	0.9	1.0	0.0	1.0
Japan	1.7	10.2	0.0	1.2
Laos	0.2	0.2	0.0	0.2
Malaysia	0.9	0.1	0.0	1.1
Myanmar	0.6	0.2	0.0	0.7
New Zealand	0.0	0.0	0.0	0.0
Philippines	0.7	0.4	0.0	0.8
Singapore	0.0	0.0	0.0	0.0
South Korea	4.8	44.7	0.3	3.1
Thailand	1.7	1.0	0.0	2.0
Vietnam	1.2	1.1	0.1	1.3

Source: Own elaboration based on UNCTAD (2021).

RCEP, Regional Comprehensive Economic Partnership.

Cambodia (3.3%) and China (2.8%). As far as broad economic sectors are concerned, the existing level of protection among the RCEP countries appears to be relatively higher in agriculture while being pretty minor for natural resources. Tariffs are also relatively significant in the manufacturing sectors, especially for Cambodia, which average import tariffs equal 4% as well as for China (3.1%) and South Korea (3.1%).

Under the RCEP Agreement, trade liberalisation will be achieved with gradual tariff reductions, allowing for considerable exemptions for sensitive and strategic sectors. Tariff concessions are ultimately to eliminate tariffs on over 90% of goods traded within RCEP. Many tariffs are to be abolished immediately, whereas others will be gradually reduced during the 20-year period. The remaining tariffs will be largely limited to strategic sectors, for each many of the RCEP countries have opted out from any liberalisation commitments. In principle, the RCEP Agreement will gradually reduce import tariffs especially with regard to China, Japan and South Korea since, in the case of other RCEP members, they are already very low.

Tariff concessions[2] vary considerably in the individual RCEP countries as indicated in Table 4.3. The concession of the countries already applying low tariffs would be necessarily lower than the concessions of the countries where the existing tariffs are higher. In the case of Australia and New Zealand, the percentage of products covered by tariff concessions is quite low, which results from the fact that almost all of these countries' tariffs are already at zero (98.6%). In turn, tariff concessions by China, Japan and South Korea are larger and wider in coverage due to relatively higher tariffs they currently apply.

Table 4.3 Tariff concessions by RCEP members

Country	*Pre-RCEP*		*RCEP concessions*		*RCEP exceptions*	
	Tariff lines with zero tariff, %	*Tariff lines with non-zero tariffs, %*	*Tariff lines for tariff reduction, %*	*Average concession, p.p.*	*Tariff lines remaining uncommitted, %*	*Average tariff on uncommitted lines*
ASEAN	91.1	8.9	3.9	9.0	5.0	20.9
Australia and New Zealand	98.6	1.4	1.0	4.9	0.4	3.6
China	71.6	28.4	19.6	9.8	8.8	16.7
Japan	79.5	20.5	8.2	7.4	12.3	32.3
South Korea	70.4	29.6	20.3	9.7	9.3	110.7

Source: Own elaboration based on UNCTAD (2021).

Table 4.4 RCEP tariff concessions, by sector

Country	*Pre-RCEP*		*RCEP concessions*		*RCEP exceptions*	
	Tariff lines with zero tariff, %	*Tariff lines with non-zero tariffs, %*	*Tariff lines for tariff reduction, %*	*Average concession, p.p.*	*Tariff lines remaining uncommitted, %*	*Average tariff on uncommitted lines*
Agriculture	75	25.2	8.4	12.8	16.8	69.8
Natural resources	90	10.0	4.5	4.8	5.5	13.7
Manufacturing	91	9.4	5.5	8.0	3.9	14.5

Source: Own elaboration based on Nicita (2021).

On average, RCEP tariff concessions by China and South Korea cover about 20% of their HS 6-digit lines[3] for an average reduction of almost 10 p.p. Japan's tariff concessions are considerably smaller than concessions by China and South Korea, both in coverage and magnitude, equalling 8.2%. However, the three major economies remained uncommitted to liberalise tariffs on a substantial share of HS 6-digit products (12.3% for Japan, 9.3% for South Korea and 8.8% for China). Average tariffs on these products are substantially high, especially for South Korea (110.7).

Additionally, RCEP tariff concessions vary across sectors. The concessions in agriculture are particularly important since they will result in a tariff reduction of 12.8 p.p. in 8.4% of products. However, the agricultural sector remains relatively more protected with a relatively high number of uncommitted tariff lines – 16.8% of tariff lines remaining uncommitted for agriculture versus 3.9% for manufacturing (Table 4.4). Among the natural resources sector, trade among RCEP members was already largely liberalised, with about 90% of HS 6-digit products already facing zero tariffs. Still, RCEP tariff concessions will result in an average reduction of about 4.8 p.p. in about 4.5% of natural resources products. The manufacturing sector is also largely already liberalised, as 91% of HS 6-digit products have a zero tariff. Even so, RCEP is further liberalising the manufacturing sector by bringing an average reduction of about 8 p.p. in the 5.5% of tariff lines that have been committed to liberalisation. RCEP commitments will leave only 4% of lines uncommitted.

It can be concluded that RCEP commitments substantially reduce tariffs among the RCEP members, but only in a limited number of products and countries and in bilateral trade flows. This is largely due to the fact that the majority of trade has already been liberalised under the MFN or other trade agreements, as well as owing to the considerable number of lines uncommitted to liberalisation under RCEP. Moreover, the RCEP countries have opted out of any commitment in the case of a number of sensitive and strategic sectors. On the one hand, tariff concessions on agriculture are substantial, but on the other hand, the sector remains relatively protected because of the large number of uncommitted products.

To conclude, RCEP has several significant attributes. First of all, RCEP is a modern agreement, not only updating the coverage of the existing ASEAN+1 FTAs, but also taking into account the changing and emerging trade realities, including the age of electronic commerce, the potential of micro, small and medium enterprises, the deepening regional value chain and the complexity of market competition. It will complement WTO, building on the WTO Agreement, in the areas where the signatories have agreed to update or go beyond its provisions.

Secondly, RCEP is a comprehensive agreement in several dimensions. In terms of the scope and depth of commitments, it comprises provisions, which, beyond trade in goods, also cover a great number of other issues, such as, e.g., trade in services, investment, e-commerce, IPRs and competition policy. Thirdly, analysing the coverage of RCEP, it is one of the world's largest FTA in terms of GDP, merchandise trade and population. Additionally, the novel element is that RCEP establishes new trade relations to evolve under a single FTA; it allows China and Japan, as well as Japan and South Korea to be part of the same FTA. If India had not dropped out in the final year of negotiations, RCEP would allow India to establish its trade relations through a contractual agreement with a substantial number of East Asian countries.

When it comes to RCEP's weaknesses, the analyses showed that it has less extensive commitments than CPTPP, though they both seek to reduce trade barriers and establish common rules and standards. In terms of market access, CPTPP will eliminate tariffs on a greater number of tariff lines (99%) and reduce barriers to trade in services for more sectors. This is in part due to CPTPP's uniform negative list approach, compared to RCEP's hybrid approach. There are also differences in rulemaking, with RCEP not covering some CPTPP issues, like SOEs, labour and environmental standards, and covering other issues, but with less extensive (e.g., IPR) or enforceable (e.g., investment, digital trade) commitments.

4.3 CPTPP and RCEP – current and potential economic effects

RCEP as well as CPTPP unite a diverse group of countries, which indicates considerable economic heterogeneity, in terms of overall size, level of development and economic structures. For example, within RCEP, in 2023, China's GDP reached US$ 17.2 trillion whereas Brunei's GDP reached only US$ 13.2 billion. In turn, within CPTPP, Japan indicates the highest GDP, reaching US$ 4.6 trillion and Brunei is again the country with the lowest value of this indicator.

Analysing the combined GDP of RCEP and CPTPP, it is notable that the former considerably surpasses the latter. In 2023, the share of RCEP's GDP reached 31% of global GDP, whereas the share of CPTPP's global GDP was two and a half times smaller (Figures 4.1 and 4.2). Since the beginning of East Asian institutionalisation processes, i.e., 1997, a growth in the share of RCEP's GDP in global GDP by 10.4 p.p. has been recorded. It was largely attributed to a considerable increase of China's GDP share in global GDP, but also ASEAN countries and South Korea extended their shares between 1997 and 2023. However, over the past decades, the share of CPTPP's GDP in global GDP has declined by 4.6 p.p. It was mainly caused by the fact that

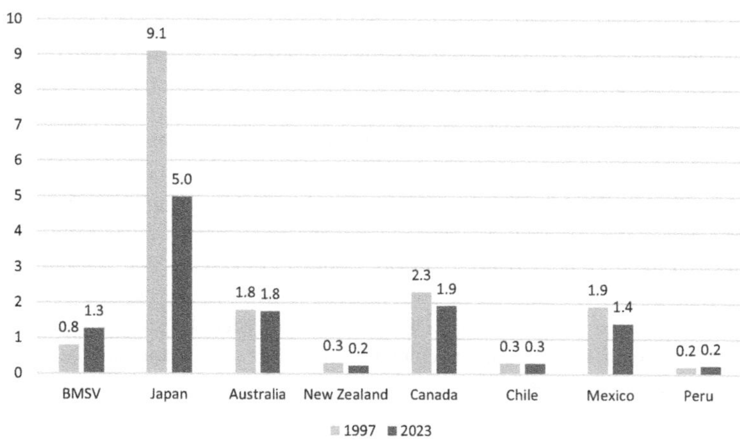

Figure 4.1 The share of Comprehensive and Progressive Agreement for Trans-Pacific Partnership's (CPTPP's) GDP in world GDP (constant 2015 US$) (%).

Source: Own elaboration based on World Development Indicators (2024).

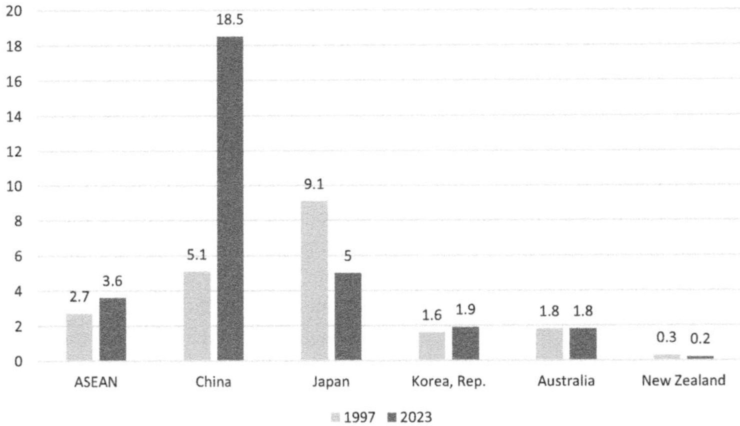

Figure 4.2 The share of Regional Comprehensive Economic Partnership's (RCEP's) GDP in world GDP (constant 2015 US$) (%).

Source: Own elaboration based on World Development Indicators (2024).

Japan has decreased its share by 4.1 p.p. Also, Canada and Mexico's GDP share in global GDP shrank in the period 1997–2023. Currently, the biggest contributor within CPTPP's GDP is Japan (5%), followed by Canada (1.9%) and Mexico (1.4%). Within RCEP's GDP, China is the most significant country in terms of the GDP share in global GDP (18.5%), followed by Japan (5%) and ASEAN countries (3.6%).

Also, in terms of international trade, there are also discrepancies among member countries of both regional trade arrangements. Within RCEP, China records the highest trade turnovers; in 2023, its total exports and imports almost reached US$ 6 trillion, whereas in Laos and Brunei, the total trade volume was almost 400 times lower. In turn, within CPTPP, Japan's trade turnovers were almost 100 times higher than in Brunei. Many of the East Asian economies are already well integrated with each other through trade and investment, through the existing economic agreements as ASEAN and through the growth of regional supply chains in East Asia. For example, in 2020, the share of intra-RCEP exports accounted for over 38% of its total exports and the share of intra-RCEP imports exceeded 47% of its total imports; however, CPTPP's intra-regional trade is less significant than the trade exchange within the RCEP area. The analysis of intra-trade intensity of the East Asian economies within RCEP has revealed that, in 1997–2021, their trade was targeted at the region (Suska, 2023), however, to a different extent. Although contributing less in terms of value, the smaller countries' trade is relatively more dependent on RCEP. For example, 90% of Lao's, 82% of Myanmar's and 72% of Brunei's total trade are with other RCEP countries. On the contrary, China's trade with RCEP countries is more modest in relative terms

(22% of China's total trade was within RCEP in 2021); similarly, Japan (35%) and South Korea (45%) also indicate lower trade integration with the RCEP countries. Lower values of intra-RCEP trade, especially in China, but also Japan and South Korea, result from the fact that they are largely dependent on extra-regional trade. In turn, China and Japan as well as several other RCEP countries are particularly well integrated in global trade networks, including South Korea, Singapore, Australia, Thailand and nowadays increasingly Vietnam. The trade exchange is also crucial for many smaller, less-developed economies in the region, which have relatively high trade shares in relation to GDP and which perceive integration in regional supply chains as a path to achieve economic success.

Carrying out the analysis of world trade at the level of CPTPP and RCEP, it can be observed that countries within the RCEP area recorded bigger share in world trade than CPTPP members throughout the entire 1997–2023 period. Currently, the RCEP's share in world trade is almost twice the CPTPP's share, amounting to 27.1% and 14.7%, respectively (2023). As Figures 4.3 and 4.4 show, since 1997, RCEP has consistently been increasing its share in world trade; in world exports it rose from 21% in 1997 to 29.2% in 2023, and in world imports, from 19.1% in 1997 to 24.9% in 2023. However, RCEP's share in both world exports and imports slightly decreased in 2023 as compared to 2021. It largely resulted from the fact that China has visibly decreased its share in world trade, recently; in world exports it fell from 15.1% in 2021 to 14.2% in 2023, and in world imports, from 11.3% in 2021 to 10.6% in 2023. Also, the ASEAN countries as well as Japan and South Korea recorded a slight decrease of their share in world trade in terms of both exports and imports in 2023 as compared to 2021.

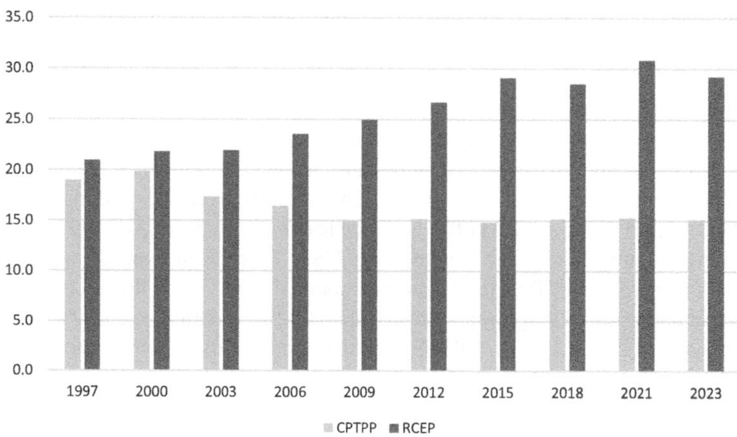

Figure 4.3 The share of CPTPP's and RCEP's exports in world exports (%).

Source: Own elaboration based on UNCTAD (2024).

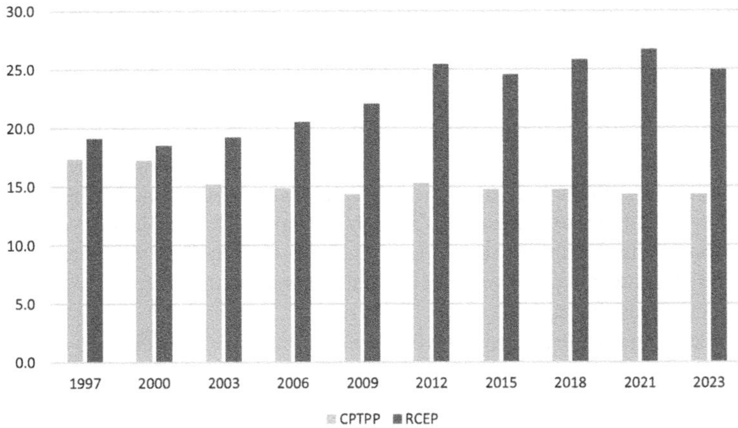

Figure 4.4 The share of CPTPP's and RCEP's imports in world imports (%).

Source: Own elaboration based on UNCTAD (2024).

In turn, the share of the CPTPP countries in world trade visibly went down in the 1997–2023 period. In 1997, in world exports it accounted for 19% and in world imports it was 17.4%, whereas in 2023, CPTPP's share in world exports and imports fell to 15.1% and 14.3%, respectively. This fall in both world exports and imports was influenced by considerable weakening of Japan's position in world trade over the past decades. Between 1997 and 2023, Japan's share in world exports decreased from 7.5% in 1997 to 3% in 2023 and its world imports, from 6% in 1997 to 3% in 2023. Additionally, Canada declined its significance in world trade, contributing to an overall decrease of CPTPP's share in world trade. Since the CPTPP Agreement entered into force in 2018, no spectacular changes in CPTPP's share in world exports and imports have been recorded; they remain nearly at the same level.

The analysis of the trade structure of CPTPP and RCEP from the East Asian perspective has revealed important changes in terms of trading partners and the composition of exports and imports over the past decades. As Figure 4.5 shows, CPTPP's geographical trade structure, in 1997, was strongly dominated by one country – the USA. In terms of exports, in 1997, the US share in CPTPP's total exports amounted to 41.3%, followed by East Asian countries – Hong Kong (4.6%), Japan (4.2%), South Korea (3.9%) and Singapore (3.8%). In turn, CPTPP imported most goods also from the USA; the US share in CPTPP's total imports accounted for 36.4% in 1997. Other significant CPTPP's import partners were Japan (6.8%), China (6.3%), Malaysia (3.70%) and Germany (3.5%). Nowadays, except for the USA, also China dominates CPTPP's trade structure (Figure 4.6). Whereas the USA has decreased its significance as a key trade partner, China has strengthened its

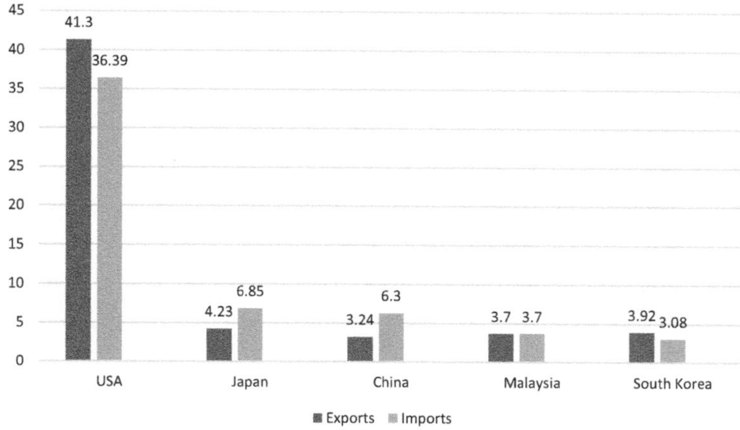

Figure 4.5 Geographical structure of CPTPP's trade in 1997 (%).

Source: Own elaboration based on UN Comtrade Database (2022).

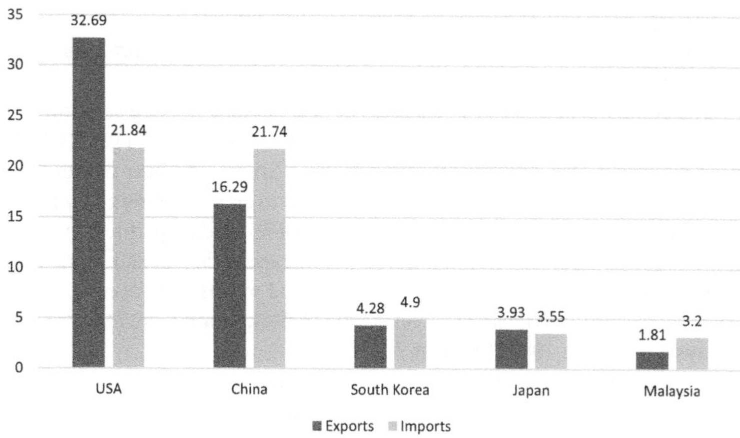

Figure 4.6 Geographical structure of CPTPP's trade in 2021 (%).

Source: Own elaboration based on UN Comtrade Database (2022).

position in CPTPP's trade structure, increasing its share in CPTPP's exports from 3.2% in 1997 to 16.3% in 2023, and in CPTPP's imports, from 6.3% in 1997 to 21.7% in 2023. It is notable that currently CPTPP's imports is dominated by two trading partners, the USA and China, which occupy an equally important position in CPTPP's geographical trade structure. Attention also attracts South Korea, which considerably expanded its trade with the CPTPP

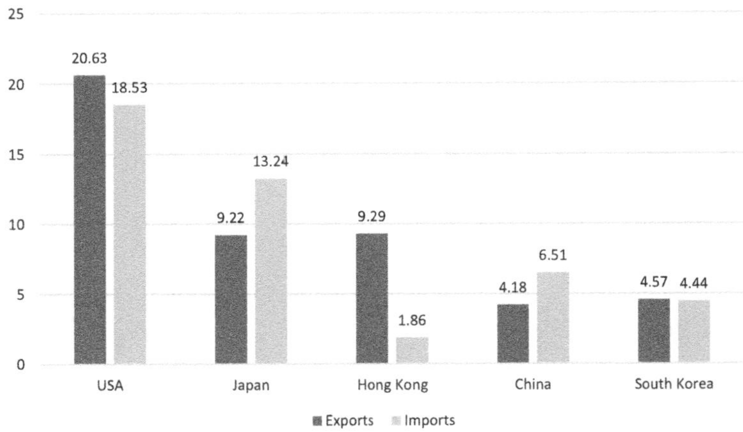

Figure 4.7 Geographical structure of RCEP's trade in 1997 (%).

Source: Own elaboration based on UN Comtrade Database (2022).

countries, overtaking Japan, and becoming CPTPP's third most important trading partner, with the share equalling 4.3% of CPTPP's exports and 4.9% of CPTPP's imports in 2023.

The comparison of CPTPP's and RCEP's geographical trade structure reveals that the latter has been more diversified. Similar to CPTPP, RCEP's most important trading partner has been the USA for the past decades. In 1997, the US share in RCEP's exports amounted to 20.6%, followed by Hong Kong (9.3%) and Japan (9.2%). The list of "top five" trading partners in terms of CPTPP's exports was complemented by Singapore (5.4%) and South Korea (4.6%). In turn, the RCEP countries imported most goods from the USA (18.5%), followed by Japan (13.2%), China (6.5%), South Korea (4.4%) and Malaysia (4.2%) in 1997 (Figure 4.7).

Currently RCEP's trade structure is dominated by two countries: RCEP's exports – by the USA and China, and RCEP's imports – by China and the USA (Figure 4.8). Although the USA is still currently the most important trading partner in the RCEP area (in 2021, RCEP's trade exchange with the USA reached US$ 146,356 trillion and with China reached US$ 139,943 trillion), over the past decades, it has considerably been decreasing its significance in RCEP's geographical trade structure, whereas China's position has practically remained unchanged. Nowadays, in terms of exports, the USA is still RCEP's most important trading partner, with the share accounted for 15.5% of RCEP's total exports, followed by China (10.5%), Hong Kong (8%), Japan (5.2%) and South Korea (4.4%). In turn, RCEP imports most goods from China (in 2021, RCEP's imports from China accounted for 12.7% of its total imports), followed by the USA (8.1%), Japan (6.8%), South Korea (6.4%) and Malaysia

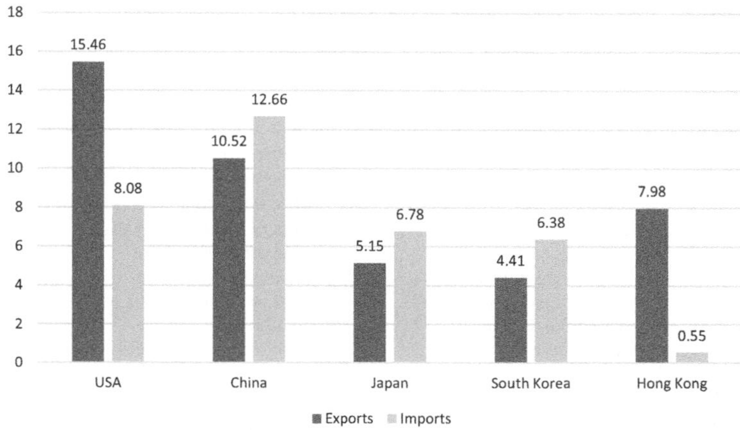

Figure 4.8 Geographical structure of RCEP's trade in 2021 (%).

Source: Own elaboration based on UN Comtrade Database (2022).

(5.2%). It is also notable that, between 1997 and 2021, Japan recorded a substantial decrease in RCEP's total trade and was undertaken by China in terms of both exports and imports.

Analysing the structure of trade in goods of East Asian members of CPTPP and RCEP, it is notable that, over the past decades, it has been dominated by commodity groups representing manufactured goods, especially electrical machinery and equipment, whereas agricultural products cannot be found either in the "top five" or "top ten" list of the most traded goods. According to Visual Capitalist (2024), East Asia's top exporting category is integrated circuits. They are used in a multitude of applications spanning computing, communications, consumer electronics, automotive, industrial automation, medical devices, aerospace and defence. The leader in exporting integrated circuits is South Korea, whose exports amount to approximately US$ 121 billion per year in trade, followed by Singapore, Malaysia and the Philippines. The largest East Asian economy, China, is known for the production of a variety of products, but its top exports come from broadcasting equipment, including TVs, cameras and radios (approximately US$ 272 billion per year).

The analysis of the commodity trade structure within CPTPP reveals that indeed electrical machinery and equipment and parts thereof [HS 85] prevails, followed by nuclear reactors, boilers, machinery and mechanical appliances and parts thereof [HS 84]. However, a decrease in the share of this top exporting category can be observed, from 19.7% in 1997 to 17.5% in 2021 (Table 4.5). Also, the share of nuclear reactors, boilers, machinery and mechanical appliances and parts thereof [HS 84], ranked as the second in CPTPP's commodity structure, fell from 18.1% in 1997 to 11.5% in 2021 in

Table 4.5 Commodity structure of CPTPP's exports (%)

1997		*2021*	
Commodity group, HS 2-digit	*%*	*Commodity group, HS 2-digit*	*%*
[85] Electrical machinery and equipment and parts thereof	19.7	[85] Electrical machinery and equipment and parts thereof	17.5
[84] Nuclear reactors, boilers, machinery and mechanical appliances; parts thereof	18.1	[84] Nuclear reactors, boilers, machinery and mechanical appliances; parts thereof	11.5
[87] Vehicles; other than railway or tramway rolling stock, and parts and accessories thereof	14	[27] Mineral fuels, mineral oils and products of their distillation	10.1
[27] Mineral fuels, mineral oils and products of their distillation	6.3	[87] Vehicles; other than railway or tramway rolling stock, and parts and accessories thereof	9.5
[90] Optical, photographic, cinematographic, measuring, checking, medical or surgical instruments and apparatus; parts and accessories	3.4	[26] Ores, slag and ash	6.2
Other	38.5	other	45.2

Source: Own elaboration based on UN Comtrade Database (2022).

HS, Harmonised System.

CPTPP's total exports. Additionally, vehicles other than railway or tramway rolling stock and parts and accessories thereof [HS 87] have weakened their position in the CPTPP's export structure, whereas CPTPP has expanded exports of mineral fuels, mineral oils and products of their distillation [HS 27], which increased from 6.3% in 1997 to 10.1% in 2021.

Analysing the CPTPP's structure of imported goods, it is notable that it is also dominated by electrical machinery and equipment and parts thereof [HS 85] and nuclear reactors, boilers, machinery and mechanical appliances and parts thereof [HS 84]; however, the share of the former increased from 17.1% in 1997 to 19.2% in 2021, whereas the share of the latter decreased from 15.6% in 1997 to 12.5% in 2021 (Table 4.6). In CPTPP's import structure, an important place is also occupied by mineral fuels, mineral oils and products of their distillation [HS 27] (12.5% in 2021) as well as vehicles, other than railway or tramway rolling stock and parts and accessories thereof [HS 87] (6.6% in 2021). In CPTPP's trade structure by "top five" commodities, new products could be found in 2021: in terms of exports – ores, slag and ash [HS 26] (6.2%), and in terms of imports – plastics and articles thereof [HS 39] (3.8%).

The commodity structure of the East Asian countries within the RCEP area has become more diversified over the past decades and new products have

Table 4.6 Commodity structure of CPTPP's imports (%)

1997		*2021*	
Commodity group, HS 2-digit	*%*	*Commodity group, HS 2-digit*	*%*
[85] Electrical machinery and equipment and parts thereof	17.1	[85] Electrical machinery and equipment and parts thereof	19.2
[84] Nuclear reactors, boilers, machinery and mechanical appliances; parts thereof	15.6	[84] Nuclear reactors, boilers, machinery and mechanical appliances; parts thereof	12.5
[27] Mineral fuels, mineral oils and products of their distillation	10	[27] Mineral fuels, mineral oils and products of their distillation	12.2
[87] Vehicles; other than railway or tramway rolling stock	7.7	[87] Vehicles; other than railway or tramway rolling stock, and parts and accessories thereof	6.6
[90] Optical, photographic, cinematographic, measuring, checking, precision, medical or surgical instruments and apparatus; parts and accessories	3.1	[39] Plastics and articles thereof	3.8
Other	46.4	other	45.8

Source: Own elaboration based on UN Comtrade Database (2022).

gained in significance in terms of both exports and imports. Since 1997, the most important position in the export structure of RCEP, similar to CPTPP, has been occupied by electrical machinery and equipment and parts thereof [HS 85], with the share equalling 24.5% in 2021, followed by nuclear reactors, boilers, machinery and mechanical appliances and parts thereof [HS 84] (14.1%) (Table 4.7). In 2021, vehicles, other than railway or tramway rolling stock and parts and accessories thereof [HS 87], improved their position in RCEP's export structure in comparison to 1997, although their share decreased from 9.7% in 1997 to 5.4% in 2021. In the commodity structure by five most important products exported by RCEP, a new commodity group can be found, namely plastics and articles thereof [HS 39].

As far as RCEP's imports are concerned, an increase in the share of electrical machinery and equipment and parts thereof [HS 85] was recorded from 17.9% in 1997 to 22.8% in 2021 (Table 4.8). Apart from this commodity group, an important place in RCEP's import structure is occupied by mineral fuels, mineral oils and products of their distillation [HS 27] (15.1% in 2021) and nuclear reactors, boilers, machinery and mechanical appliances and parts thereof [HS 84] (10.1% in 2021). Within RCEP's "top five" imported goods, a new category appeared in 2021 – ores, slag and ash [HS 26], accounting for 5.9% of RCEP's imports.

Table 4.7 Commodity structure of RCEP's exports (%)

1997		*2021*	
Commodity group, HS 2-digit	*%*	*Commodity group, HS 2-digit*	*%*
[85] Electrical machinery and equipment and parts thereof	24.4	[85] Electrical machinery and equipment and parts thereof	24.5
[84] Machinery and mechanical appliances; parts thereof	19.7	[84] Nuclear reactors, boilers, machinery and mechanical appliances; parts thereof	14.1
[99] Other products	15.6	[87] Vehicles; other than railway or tramway rolling stock, and parts and accessories thereof	5.4
[87] Vehicles; other than railway or tramway rolling stock, and parts and accessories thereof	9.7	[27] Mineral fuels, mineral oils and products of their distillation	4.6
[27] Mineral fuels, mineral oils and products of their distillation	5.9	[39] Plastics and articles thereof	3.6
Other	24.7	other	47.8

Source: Own elaboration based on UN Comtrade Database (2022).

Table 4.8 Commodity structure of RCEP's imports (%)

1997		*2021*	
Commodity group, HS 2-digit	*%*	*Commodity group, HS 2-digit*	*%*
[85] Electrical machinery and equipment and parts thereof	17.9	[85] Electrical machinery and equipment and parts thereof	22.8
[84] Nuclear reactors, boilers, machinery and mechanical appliances; parts thereof	15.5	[27] Mineral fuels, mineral oils and products of their distillation; bituminous substances; mineral waxes	15.1
[27] Mineral fuels, mineral oils and products of their distillation	12.6	[84] Nuclear reactors, boilers, machinery and mechanical appliances; parts thereof	10.1
[87] Vehicles; other than railway or tramway rolling stock, and parts and accessories thereof	3.4	[26] Ores, slag and ash	5.9
[90] Optical, photographic, cinematographic, measuring, checking, medical or surgical instruments and apparatus; parts and accessories	3.1	[87] Vehicles; other than railway or tramway rolling stock, and parts and accessories thereof	3.7
Other	47.6	other	42.4

Source: Own elaboration based on UN Comtrade Database (2022).

The presented above analyses reveal that important changes have occurred in macroeconomic performance of the CPTPP and RCEP members. RCEP economies have been increasing their share in global GDP, also ASEAN countries have been gaining in importance in the global economy. Additionally, RCEP has consistently been expanding its share in world trade (exports and imports). In contrast, CPTPP has weakened its position in the global economy in terms of GDP and international trade over the past decades, which is largely attributed to decreasing macroeconomic outcomes in Japan. Nevertheless, in the literature, the projections for both CPTPP and RCEP in terms of aggregate economic gains are quite optimistic. According to the simulation by Ferrantino, Maliszewska and Taran's (2019), increased GDP and trade flows are expected within CPTPP and RCEP. The former will increase the overall members' GDP by 0.4%, as compared to baseline scenario for 2030, and the latter by 1.5%. As far as the individual countries' performance is concerned, all CPTPP members will experience estimated GDP increases, with the highest, in percentage terms, for Brunei Darussalam (1.9%), Vietnam (1.1%), Peru (1.0%) and Malaysia (1.0%). The largest estimated gains from RCEP are for China, both in absolute terms ($438 billion against a 2030 baseline) and in relative terms (2.0% of GDP). Within RCEP, other significant gainers will be Brunei (1.7% of GDP), South Korea (1.7%), India (1.7), Malaysia (0.8%) and Japan (0.7%).

Ferrantino, Maliszewska and Taran's (2019) projected that trade liberalisation under CPTPP and RCEP will facilitate an increase in exports of both regional institutional arrangements, ranging from 2.8% for CPTPP to 4.9% for RCEP. In turn, estimated increases in imports for members range from 2.7% for CPTPP to 4.9% for RCEP. The highest percentage increase in exports will be observed in New Zealand (6.4%), Vietnam (5%) and Malaysia (4.6%) under CPTPP, and in Japan (10.3%), India (7%) and New Zealand (6.2%) under RCEP. As far as changes in the commodity trade structure of CPTPP and RCEP are concerned, the highest growth of exports is projected to occur in food and beverages, wearing apparel and textiles due to a relatively high reduction in tariffs and non-tariff barriers for these commodity groups. Ferrantino, Maliszewska and Taran's (2019) remarked that increases in trade for CPTPP and RCEP are projected to be significantly larger than any trade diversion observed by non-members. Gains in total exports of CPTPP and RCEP members are also much higher compared to exports losses of non-members, exceeding them in more than five times. As a result, both CPTPP and RCEP are expected to boost the global exports, with the larger FTA having a greater positive impact on global trade.

In turn, according to Petri and Plummer's (2020a) projection, RCEP will add US$ 209 billion annually to world incomes, and US$ 500 billion to world trade by 2030. Southeast Asia will benefit significantly from RCEP (US$ 19 billion annually by 2030) but less so than Northeast Asia because it already has FTAs with RCEP partners.

Following computer simulations in a related study also by Petri and Plummer (2020b), CPTPP and RCEP will raise global national incomes in 2030 by an annual US$ 147 billion and US$ 186 billion, respectively. They both will yield especially large benefits for China, Japan and South Korea, and losses for the USA and India. The authors also argued that RCEP will be especially valuable since it strengthens East Asian integration, raising trade among members by US$ 428 billion and reducing trade among non-members by US$ 48 billion. Additionally, Petri and Plummer's (2020b) simulation showed that RCEP and CPTPP could together more than offset the global negative economic effects of the China-US trade war, but not the individual losses of China and the USA. Moreover, the incremental value of CPTPP will be reduced by the trade war (from US$ 147 billion to US$ 121 billion) while the value of RCEP will be increased (from US$ 186 billion to US$ 209 billion). The authors also projected that RCEP will be economically significant with or without India, and more significant than CPTPP, with especially important gains for China, Japan and Korea.

4.4 RCEP and CPTPP – opportunities and threats for Europe

At the beginning of the third decade of the 21st century, the EU faced a need to revise (again) its trade policy strategy challenged by, among others, US protectionist measures, China's growing assertiveness, rising economic nationalism worldwide and the negative impact of the COVID-19 pandemic. Additionally, the EU's markets were confronted with two mega-FTAs – CPTPP and RCEP. As a response, a new trade policy strategy, initiated by the Trade Policy Review (TPR), was developed in 2021 (European Commission, 2021). Under the TPR, the EU still maintains its liberal commitment to trade openness and reforming WTO across all its functions but also reserves the right to defend and pursue its economic and political interests by means of trade policy. The EU's trade policy has a number of distinctive features, which might be relevant for East Asia, RCEP and CPTPP, such as:

- Requirements concerning the depth of trade agreements. FTAs should go far beyond mere tariff removals but also embrace RoOs, services and IPRs, including geographical indications, industrial and agricultural, standards, public procurement, subsidies and competition, sustainability and regulatory cooperation.
- Promoting and enforcing European (and international) rules and standards through trade agreements (e.g., RoOs, technical standards and regulations in industry, food safety, services, IPRs, data protection and sustainability).
- Promoting and respecting European values. While trade and political agreements are parallelly concluded, the EU expects their partners to respect values and standards associated with the value of human rights, the rule of law and liberal democracy.

- Separation of trade and investment. The EU does not negotiate trade and investment protection agreements together any longer.
- Commitment to the rule-based multilateral trading system (despite its competitive bilateralism and the crisis of WTO and WTO DS mechanism).

The EU has always encountered certain reservations in relations with Asia, resulting, to a large extent, from the colonial past but also from the fact the EU can be a difficult (and demanding) partner. It should be emphasised here that Europe's natural priority is Europe and not Asia or other regions. This may partially explain why Europe's interactions with Asia have been rather passive and lacking strategic directions. Although Europe and Asia initiated the Asia-Europe Meeting (ASEM) process based on interregional dialogue and cooperation in 1996, which has contributed to bring both regions closer to each other and enhance mutual understanding, it has been criticised as an insignificant forum that does not bring concrete outcomes or solutions to current problems. Nevertheless, the 13th ASEM Summit held in 2021 successfully ended with the reaffirmation of the comprehensive partnership between Asia and Europe. The leaders resolved to work together for peace and security, inclusive and sustainable development, resilience and prosperity and the promotion and protection of human rights, on the basis of the UN Charter to accelerate progress towards the sustainable development goals (ASEM, 2021).

Despite the Europe's relatively slow and sometimes inadequate reaction to Asia's economic dynamism, over the past decades, the intensification of intra-regional trade and economic integration between both regions has been observed. An empirical look at merchandise trade shows how close the economic relations between Europe and the Asia-Pacific have become. In 2019, the EU's major trading partner region for exports and imports was East Asia and the Pacific. The EU's exports and imports to this region accounted for 25% and 35% of the total EU's international trade, respectively. While analysing the EU's five most significant trading partners (outside the EU), with regard to the extra-EU exports, China ranked second, with a share of 11% (behind the USA), and in terms of the extra-EU imports, China is the first supplier of its goods, with the share of 20% (followed by the USA) (Suska, 2022). Except for China, other East Asian economies with quite significant trading relations to the EU are Japan and South Korea. Additionally, Hong Kong, Indonesia, Singapore, Thailand and Vietnam can be counted among the EU's relevant trading partners in the region of East Asia.

The role and significance of trade between the EU and the Asia-Pacific is also visible in the case of RCEP. EU's exports to RCEP countries have risen from over 13% to nearly 19% of total extra-EU exports since the beginning of the new millennium. Nevertheless, the RCEP Agreement has received some (but not intense) attention in Europe; though, the opinions on its significance for Europe are different. Proponents of the agreement emphasised the future growth potential of trade and investment integration within the RCEP area, whereas sceptics pointed to its overall shallow scope and lengthy transition periods. There were also voices that warned from its discriminatory effects for European economy and businesses (Politico, 2020; Gabriel and Scharping, 2022).

Undisputedly, by liberalising trade and harmonising RoOs, RCEP promotes intra-regional trade, but also affects trade with third countries, including the EU. For exporting countries, the total trade effect is made of trade diversion and trade creation. According to the theory of economics, beneficiaries of the tariff reduction enjoy both the positive diversion effect and the positive creation effect while all other partners will suffer from the negative diversion effect and no trade creation effect. The discrimination of imports from third countries and their substitution by (less efficient) imports within the RCEP area may be harmful for the EU as its exports to RCEP countries accounts for one-fifth of its total exports. However, the trade diversion effect should vary, depending on the exposure to tariff liberalisation of individual RCEP countries. ASEAN countries, Australia and New Zealand have already liberalised their trade under bilateral FTAs; hence, serious trade distortions would rather not happen in these markets because of concluding the RCEP Agreement. However, the tariff liberalisation in China-Japan-South Korea trade could be harmful for European exporters, especially with regard to China – the biggest importer of EU's goods within RCEP – as Japan and South Korea will benefit from tariff reductions for their exports to China and the EU will not. Already, the empirical analysis revealed that EU's exports to China (but also Japan and South Korea) as a share of its total exports have decreased since the RCEP Agreement came into force.

On the other hand, scholars, who estimated the total trade and income effects of RCEP on the European economy (e.g., Park et al., 2021; Nicita, 2021), argued that Europe will benefit from rising import demand of RCEP countries and slightly lower export prices due to a more efficient production system within the RCEP area. The resulting welfare effects are expected, thus, to be positive.

Besides the static and income effects mentioned above, also dynamic effects (e.g., on supply chains, foreign investment, economic growth) should be highlighted, which may turn significant in a longer perspective. From European perspective, in the long run, the region with the RCEP Agreement will become more attractive; however, RCEP companies will also increase their competitiveness in world markets. Hence, European companies will have to react to the changes brought about by RCEP. One of the responses may be increasing foreign direct investment in RCEP countries, especially the ones the EU has already concluded bilateral FTAs with (i.e., Japan, New Zealand, Singapore, South Korea and Vietnam) and is likely to conclude with (e.g., Indonesia and the Philippines). RCEP countries can assure a relatively easy and reliable market access as well as a relatively stable and resilient investment environment for European businesses. The relatively liberal RoO will allow for the value-added from European sources, thus facilitating the participation of European companies in RCEP markets.

On the other hand, Asia's industrial and growth dynamics, enhanced by market and institutionalised regional integration, may pose a threat for Europe's economic and technological competitiveness. EU-based businesses (as stemming from the third countries) have only limited access to regional trade and innovation networks and may be late to important new industrial and technological developments. If European companies do not respond to the new trends in Asia, then their market position may quickly worsen.

Although RCEP is a shallow agreement in comparison to EU's bilateral FTAs or CPTPP, it is not just another trade agreement since its size gives it the potential to shape global trade patterns and rules, including the multilateral trading system and WTO centrality. It may fundamentally change the balance of power in international trade policy, shifting the international trade gravity towards the Asia-Pacific, thus posing a challenge for the EU as the major trading power. Thus, the establishment of the RCEP area has significant political implications for the EU's trade (and foreign) policy, such as:

- It is surprising that the recent TPR (European Commission, 2021) does not address the EU's trade policy towards Asia (but also the Indo-Pacific); in particular, in the new EU trade policy strategy, these regions remain virtually unmentioned despite its economic and growth dynamism. If the EU aims to maintain the rule-based trading system with WTO in its centre, then closer cooperation with economies in East Asia and the Asia-Pacific seems inevitable. European countries that are outside the EU appear more flexible and responsive in their trade policies towards Asia, which can be illustrated by, e.g., the UK's accession to CPTPP as well as Georgia, Iceland and Switzerland's FTAs with China.
- The EU's reaction to the establishment of the RCEP area can obviously be concluding bilateral FTAs with individual RCEP countries to mitigate the negative effect of trade diversion. In bilateral negotiations, the EU could better promote its commercial interests, core standards and values (e.g., human rights, sustainable development and the rule of law). Therefore, currently, the EU seems not interested in direct negotiations with RCEP as a group. This option is, however, not risk-free; negotiations with individual RCEP members can be lengthy, and their outcome cannot be foreseen.
- Another strategic option for the EU can be looking at the region as a whole instead of perceiving it through individual member countries. It could be realised by strengthening the EU-ASEAN trade and investment relations and revitalising the negotiations on the establishment of EU-ASEAN agreement, which remains a long-term objective of both parties. Moreover, Europe should consider establishing direct links with RCEP and CPTPP to address important issues, such as, e.g., the management of the

implementation and enforcement of trade rules and standards or the co-existence of mega-regionalism and the multilateral trading system and WTO centrality.

- Recognising the depth of the CPTPP Agreement and its relevance for the development of future trade rules and standards, the EU could consider free trade negotiations with this Asia-Pacific trade bloc. The EU has already FTAs with eight of the 11 CPTPP countries (Canada, Chile, Japan, Mexico, New Zealand, Peru, Singapore and Vietnam) and is negotiating with one more – Australia. Only Brunei and Malaysia are so far outside the negotiations.
- The benefits from EU-CPTPP agreement would be substantial for both parties (but also for third countries). The improvement of the market access is not the only advantage. Due to the fact that the WTO reform is not within reach now, the EU-CPTPP alignment could be a good option for securing or modernising the multilateral system. Moreover, the EU could establish its firm economic and political presence in the Asia-Pacific region. For the CPTPP countries, the EU could serve as an anchor for regional integration – the role which was initially assigned to the USA.
- The substantial benefits from linking the EU to CPTPP might be countered by considerable obstacles and concerns. The implementation of such an agreement would be difficult for Europe since trade liberalisation and trade rules applied by both parties diverge significantly in several respects. It might be difficult to reach an agreement on some sensitive issues, such as, e.g., trade in agricultural goods, digital trade, data protection, DS mechanism or government procurement. Nevertheless, the potential advantage from the EU-CPTPP agreement seems to be worth the efforts to overcome the hardships.

Notes

1 The text of the CPTPP Agreement can be found on https://www.mfat.govt.nz/en/trade/free-trade-agreements/free-trade-agreements-in-force/cptpp/comprehensive-and-progressive-agreement-for-trans-pacific-partnership-text-and-resources/#bookmark0.

2 RCEP tariff concessions are detailed in Annex I "Schedules of Tariff Commitments" of the RCEP Agreement, https://www.dfat.gov.au/trade/agreements/in-force/rcep/rcep-text.

3 In the "Schedules of Tariff Commitments", the RCEP countries' tariff concessions are detailed up to the 10-digit of the Harmonised System (HS). However, the HS for classifying goods is internationally harmonised at the 6-digit level. Therefore, the analysis aggregates the data at the HS 6-digit categorisation, comprising approx. 5,300 articles/product descriptions (Nicita, 2021).

Summary and Conclusions

An increasing dynamics and transformation of integration processes in East Asia and the related threats, as well as growing significance of the entire East Asian region in international relations and the world economy, together with the redefinition of global order, accompanied by the emergence of more powerful and prosperous China, and eventually, the importance attached to economic integration in empirical research not only on East Asia, but also on other world's regions have justified the choice of the topic of this monography. In the literature, economic integration has been studied from many different theoretical and conceptual perspectives. Consequently, a great volume of elaborations dedicated to different aspects of integration, transformation and developmental processes in East Asia and the Pacific was created. However, an in-depth review of the studies on economic integration in East Asia has highlighted certain gaps. Namely, there is a shortage of theoretical and empirical studies on East Asia's institutionalised economic integration, embodied by the recent establishment of two mega-regional trade arrangement – Regional Comprehensive Economic Partnership (RCEP) and Comprehensive and Progressive Agreement for Trans-Pacific Partnership (CPTPP). Their actual and potential impact on East Asian economies, as well as on countries/institutions in other parts of the world, especially Europe and the European Union (EU), has been scarcely and vaguely researched. Hence, this monography aims to fill, at least partially, this gap in literature. Its originality is reflected by the up-to-date nature of the researched topics and processes (it addresses a relevant subject area not only for East Asia but also for other regions with regard to the increased significance in terms of economic and growth dynamics of East Asian countries these days) as well as multidisciplined approach (it is embedded in the theory and practice of political science and economics).

The aim of the monography was to present regional economic integration and its institutionalisation pursued in East Asia from the European perspective and their consequences for Europe and the EU. Following the realisation of the aforementioned aim, the theoretical research on the subject matter was conducted, which was then supplemented by the empirical analysis. Eventually, the conducted studies allowed the author to draw conclusions regarding

DOI: 10.4324/9781003544234-5

East Asia's institutionalised regionalism, its economic effects and make implications for the economic policy.

The analyses provided in Chapter 1 dedicated to theoretical concepts of integration from the political science, social and economic perspective allowed for the formulation of fundamental assumptions for economic integration. The theory of pluralism perceives integration through the prism of respect for international peace and national security, together with the policy of strategic diplomatic actions as well as the conviction that the state is a foundation for political life. Federalism assumes that integration is based on the centralisation of particular functions at the federal level and decentralisation at the regional and local level to ensure the full participation of a unit. According to the theory of functionalism, integration processes can be analysed from the perspective of a static structure or dynamic changes. The representatives of this approach, originating from the liberal tradition, emphasise the fact that interests are the key engine of the society, and economics is the main and the most effective means leading to integration. Neofunctionalism, in turn, puts an emphasis on the institutional arrangement and political organisation of integration, simultaneously stressing the role of political and functional spill-over. The modern theories of integration – the trajectory of the development of integration processes and liberal intergovernmentalism – formulate models/trajectories of integration processes, emphasising the growing significance of supranational and national institutions and the necessity of intergovernmental cooperation, simultaneously considering the specificity and differentiation of national preferences. Together with the change in global economic conditions, new theories of economic integration have been developed, besides the traditional ones. The driving forces behind previous integration efforts (trade creation and trade diversion) were entirely different from the factors that have curbed the recent integration development, such as private sector participation, FDI and an increasing role of services, leading ultimately to the creation of economic growth. However, the rationale behind the economic integration of developing countries cannot be explained only in terms of static and dynamic effects that determine integration processes among developed economies. Here, different aspects of developing economies should be considered, such as the level of economic development, structure of the economy, production features, demand preferences and trade regimes and policies, which are still subjected to further research.

Chapter 2 analysed the terms and concepts related to (regional) economic integration, regionalism and regionalisation as well as institutions and institutionalisation, anchoring the considerations in the theory of new institutional economics. The concluded studies revealed a wide range of different definitions as well as ambiguity and complexity in the meaning of the discussed notions and their multi-dimensional character. With regard to the subject of the monography and the research conducted, in integration processes, it was necessary to distinguish between two main, interwoven dimensions – market-driven and institution-driven economic integration. The former proceeds rather spontaneously, without the purposeful intervention of integrating economies, in conjunction with market forces, whereas the latter results from conscious efforts of participating countries to coordinate or unify economic and political activities. In such a dimension, institutional integration can be associated with regionalism. The analysis of institutionalisation processes allowed to distinguish certain characteristic features of institutions. First, they aim at setting common norms of social co-existence, including common international conventions, which regulate different areas of international relations. Institutionalisation also attempts to achieve common objectives for states or the whole international community related to, among others, economic and social development, international security, natural environment and health protection. Additionally, institutions and institutionalisation promote common values, like democracy, the rule of law and human rights. Actually, the role of institutions is hard to overestimate, since institutions, in connection with the economic policy and spatial location, are the indicators of the country's economic development. Furthermore, in the course of the studies, it was established that economic integration takes different institutional forms (e.g., free trade area, customs union, common market, economic union, complete economic integration), which are characterised by distinct advancement of cooperation and diverse depth of ties among economies, markets and individual member states. Integration processes, which occur at two levels – the level of markets and the level of economic policy – undergo a certain sequence of stages. In principle, these stages are similar in the initial and end phase; at the beginning, they start from free trade, and they ultimately end with full economic integration.

Chapter 3 of the monography addressed the specificity of East Asia's model of regional economic integration as well as its evolution toward institutionalised regionalism and the outcome in the form of bilateral and multilateral FTAs concluded in the region and outside it, considering the function of multinational enterprises (MNEs) as well as Association of Southeast Asian Nations (ASEAN) and Asia-Pacific Economic Cooperation (APEC) in institutionalisation processes. The analyses of this chapter confirmed that MNEs and regional production networks played an important role, as driving forces of East Asia's market-led economic integration, initially based on voluntary liberalisation of trade and investment in the region, which was subsequently complemented by institutionalisation processes. In the institutionalisation of regional economic integration in East Asia, different stages were distinguished, in which APEC and ASEAN played a crucial role. The studies conducted in this chapter also showed that East Asia's economic integration at the regional level lacked significant formal institutionalisation, which resulted from many reasons like the great economic, political and socio-cultural regional diversity, different approach to liberalisation determined by the adopted economic policy and political system as well as strong attachment to sovereignty and the primacy of internal institutions. On the other hand, factors impeding East Asian economic integration turned into its driving forces. Also delegating responsibilities and duties as well as authority by the governments of individual East Asian countries seemed inevitable in the face of globalisation processes and tighter interdependencies among global markets. Consequently, the traditional embrace of World Trade Organization (WTO) at the multilateral level and the concentration on informal, market-driven regional economic integration have evolved tówards the pursuit of greater institutionalisation, exemplified by the increased number of FTAs concluded within and outside the region. However, this practice turned rather impractical considering duplicating, overlapping and sometimes even contradictory mechanisms and institutions, causing the Asian "noodle bowl" effect, which sometimes instead of facilitating economic integration, even more complicate it.

The last chapter of the monography investigates East Asia's institutionalised regionalism, reflected in the establishment of mega-regional FTAs – CPTPP and RCEP. Despite of the fact that both trade agreements did not reduce the Asian "noodle bowl" effect because they do not eliminate the existing FTAs in the region, they supersede all the different bilateral partnerships and develop common rules, such as, e.g., the rules of origin. Hence, CPTPP and RCEP may be a remedy to the Asian "noodle bowl" effect due to the harmonisation of trade mechanisms and rules. The analyses conducted in this chapter also highlighted the significance of both trade blocks, especially RCEP in the regional and region-wide economic architecture. Already now, RCEP's GDP accounts for over 30% of global GDP and since 1997 this share has been consistently growing. Moreover, RCEP's share in world trade has exceeded 27% and the bloc is constantly expanding its exports and imports. Also, the projections for both CPTPP and RCEP in terms of aggregate economic gains are very promising; considerable increases in GDP and trade flows within both trade blocs are expected in future. The considerable aggregated macroeconomic performance of the East Asian members of CPTPP and RCEP makes important implications for other regions worldwide. Facing these facts, surprisingly, the recent European Commission's Trade Policy Review hardly addresses the EU's trade policy strategy towards Asia, but also the entire Indo-Pacific region.

The partial studies and analyses of the particular chapters described earlier allow for formulating conclusions of general nature. First, anchoring the model of East Asia's economic integration in the theory of integration might be challenging for various reasons. It should be emphasised that studies on integration, which laid foundations for the economic integration theory, were mainly conducted from the European perspective, together with the establishment of the European Community and subsequently the EU. Hence, it will be difficult to find the origins of East Asian integration in the theory of federalism, functionalism or neofunctionalism, although certain assumptions of these traditional theories may also be applied to integration processes advancing in East Asia. There is, so far, no single integration theory without space and time limitations, which could universally be applied to all models of integration and embrace the entire systematised knowledge in this area. Second, East Asia is a region of great economic, political and socio-cultural diversity. Especially, substantial economic disparities among the East Asian countries should be emphasised; East Asia is characterised by different pace of economic growth and level of economic development, including developed and developing countries. Therefore, studies on East Asian integration cannot be limited only to the case of developed European countries and they cannot be anchored unambiguously and solely either in traditional and new economic integration theories or in the economic theory for developing countries. Undoubtedly, East Asia has established its own, unique model of integration, different than the path of integration realised in Europe, which might be not fully comprehensible from the European perspective.

East Asia's economic integration, in contrast to Europe, is characterised by institutional weakness. As the matter of fact, the form of institutionalisation embraced by East Asia is different to allow for adherence to the East Asian principle of non-intervention into domestic affairs, the dominant emphasis on national interests and the manner of elitism. On the one hand, East Asian countries, despite earlier reluctance, supported the multilateral trading system of WTO, which culminated with China's accession in 2000; on the other hand, East Asia's economic integration simultaneously lacked significant formal institutionalisation. Even ASEAN, one of the most successful integration groupings in the region, eschewed full commitment to the abolishment of trade and non-trade barriers. Other ASEAN-based regional structures, like ASEAN Plus Three, also remain highly under-institutionalised. Also, APEC, since its creation, remains, in the first place, a consultative forum for trade and investment liberalisation, rather than the instigator of significant liberalisation.

Nevertheless, despite its institutional deficiency in a formal sense, East Asia's economic integration has been impressive in a practical sense, as indicated by the great number of bilateral and multilateral FTAs concluded in the region, contributing to the thrive of regional trade. However, over the past years, the traditional institutional equilibrium of East Asian economic cooperation, i.e., the embrace of WTO at the multilateral level and the concentration on informal, market-driven integration in the regional dimension, has evolved towards the pursuit of greater institutionalised regionalism. However, the East Asian commitment to a broader trade regime has, partially, turned impractical considering overlapping, duplicating and sometimes contradictory mechanisms and institutions, contributing to the Asian "noodle bowl" effect, which, instead of facilitating economic integration, may even more complicate it. It is difficult to clearly decide whether the newly established regional institutional arrangements – RCEP and CPTPP – will mitigate or accentuate this effect in a longer perspective since they do not eliminate regional FTAs that already exist. However, harmonising different trade rules and processes into the common ones under CPTPP and RCEP will definitely simplify the processes and procedures for each FTA and facilitate trade across the region.

Contemporarily, East Asia can be characterised by an increased level of dynamic economic cooperation and integration, especially in terms of trade, and simultaneously still relative institutional deficiency. To better discern East Asian integration processes and to work out implications for the economic policy, fostering the weaving of the regional institutional web, it is indispensable to understand the character of East Asia's economic integration as well as the specificity of the region. The enhancement of the institutionalisation of integration processes in East Asia will require strengthening regional integration structures by the creation of permanent institutions, supervising, regulating and assessing the realisation of the adopted objectives. Additionally, effective, long-standing cooperation among regional and region-wide institutions should be highlighted. Also, it is essential to develop and implement mechanisms and solutions to mitigate the disparities in the level of economic development among the individual economies in the region, striving for greater income convergence. Considering the character of the contemporary institutional architecture of the region, it is important to indicate the necessity to facilitate the already existing forms and structures of economic integration, increasing the level of their institutionalisation, rather than building new institutions, which may pose a risk of deepening the undesirable Asian "noodle bowl" effect in the region.

Growing economic and political significance of East Asia, together with advancing institutionalisation of regional economic integration and the establishment of two mega-regional trade agreements – CPTPP and RCEP – have far-fetched implications for the region, but also for other parts of the world, including Europe and the EU. The latter seems to respond to the East Asian economic dynamics as well as to CPTPP's and RCEP's potential to reorient trade and economic ties away from global linkages towards regionally focused relationships in East Asia in a slow and sometimes ineffective way. On the one hand, CPTPP and RCEP countries can assure a relatively easy and reliable market access as well as a relatively stable and resilient investment environment for European businesses, but on the other hand, East Asia's industrial and growth dynamics, enhanced by market and institutionalised regional integration, may pose a threat for Europe's economic and technological competitiveness. Actually, EU-based businesses have only limited access to regional trade and innovation networks and may be late to important new industrial and technological developments, which may quickly worsen their market position.

Although RCEP is a shallow agreement in comparison to EU's bilateral FTAs or CPTPP, it has the potential to shape global trade patterns and rules, including the multilateral trading system and WTO centrality. If the EU aims to maintain this system, then closer cooperation with the countries in the region of East Asia seems inevitable, keeping in mind that CPTPP and RCEP may fundamentally change the balance of power in international trade policy, shifting the international trade gravity towards the Asia-Pacific.

Bibliography

Abdel Jaber, T. (1971) A review article: The relevance of traditional integration theory to less developed countries, *Journal of Common Market Studies*, 9(3), pp. 254–267.

Abrego, L., Riezman, R. and Whalley, J. (2005) Computation and the theory of customs unions, *CESifo Economic Studies*, 51(1), pp. 117–132.

Alchian, A.A. and Demsetz, H. (1972) Production, information costs, and economic organization, *American Economic Review*, 62, pp. 777–795.

Alker, H. and Puchala, D.J. (1968) Trends in economic partnership: The North Atlantic area 1928–1963, in J. Singer (ed), *Quantitative international politics: Insights and evidence*, Free Press, New York.

Allais, M. (1958) Fondements Théoriques, Perspectives et Conditions d'un Marché Commun Effectif, special issue devoted to the Common Market , 68th year, January-February 1958, p. 56–99.

Allais, M. (1960) *L'Europe Unie*, Route de Prosperite, Paris.

Allen, R.L. (1961) Integration in less developed areas, *Kyklos,* 3, pp. 315–336.

Andic, F., Andic, S. and Dosser, D. (1971) *A theory of economic integration for developing countries*, George Allen & Unwin Ltd, London.

APEC (2016) Annex A: Lima Declaration on FTAAP. https://www.apec.org/meeting-papers/leaders-declarations/2016/2016_aelm/2016_annex-a (accessed: 20.09.2024).

Archer, C. (1992) *International organisations*, 2nd edition, Routledge, London.

ASEAN (2008) The ASEAN Charter, ASEAN Secretariat, Jakarta, January.

ASEM (2021) Multilateralism, growth, sustainable development & prosperity, https://aseminfoboard.org/asem_events/13th-asem-summit-asem13/ (accessed: 13.07.2024).

Asia Regional Integration Center (2022) https://aric.adb.org/fta-country (accessed: 13.07.2024).

Australian Government (2020) RCEP text, https://www.dfat.gov.au/trade/agreements/in-force/rcep/rcep-text (accessed: 05.04.2024).

Balassa, B. (1962) *The theory of economic integration*, George Allen & Unwin Ltd, London.

Balassa, B. (1965) *Economic development and integration, Centro De Estudios Monetario Latinoamericanos*, Mexico.

Balassa, B. and Stoutjesdijk, A. (1975) Economic integration among developing countries, *Journal of Common Market Studies*, 37, pp. 37–55.

Baldwin, R. (2012) WTO 2.0: global governance of supply chain trade, *CWPR Policy Insight*, 64, pp. 1–24.

Baldwin, R. and Wyplosz, C. (2009) *The economics of European integration*, 3rd edition, McGraw-Hill Education, London.

Baldwin, R., Forslid, R. and Haaland, J. (1995) *Investment creation and investment diversion: Simulation analysis of the single market programme*, NBER Working Paper no. 5364, National Bureau of Economic Research, Cambridge, MA.

Barrell, R. and Choy, A. (2003) *Economic integration and openness in Europe and East Asia*, NIESR Discussion Papers 2014, National Institute of Economic and Social Research (NIESR).

Bende-Nabende, A. (1999) *A comparative study of the ASEAN-5 economies, with development policy implications for the least developed countries*, Routledge, Abingdon and New York.

Bhagwati, J. (1971) Trade-diverting customs unions and welfare-improvement: A clarification, *The Economic Journal*, 81(323), pp. 580–587.

Bhambri, R.S. (1962) Customs unions and underdeveloped countries, *Economia Internazionale*, 15, May, pp. 237–244.

Bonn, M. (1938) *The crumbling of empire: the disintegration of world economy*, George Allen & Unwin, London.

Burfisher, M., Robinson, S. and Thierfelder, K. (2003) *Regionalism: Old and new, theory and practice*, in Paper prepared for presentation to the International Agricultural Trade Research Consortium (IATRC) Conference, Italy.

Burges, M. (1998) *Federalism and European Union: Political ideas, influences and strategies in European Community, 1972-1987*, Routledge, London.

Burges, M. (2009) *Federalism*, in A. Wiener and T. Diez, *European integration theory*, 2nd edition, Oxford University Press, Oxford, pp. 25–44.

Camilleri, J.A. (2003) *Regionalism in the new Asia-Pacific order: The political economy of the Asia-Pacific region*, vol. 2, Edward Elgar, Cheltenham-Northampton.

Campell, J.L. (2004) *Institutional change and globalization*, Princeton University Press, Princeton, NJ.

Cannadine, D. (ed.) (1990) *The speeches of Winston Churchill*, Penguin Books, London.

Caporaso, J.A. and Keeler, J.T. (1993) *The European community and regional integration theory*, University of Washington, Seattle.

Carpenter, T. (2008) A historical perspective on regionalism, in R. Baldwin and P. Low (eds), *Multilateralizing regionalism; Challenges for the global trading system*, Cambridge University Press, Cambridge.

Chacholiades, M. (1978) *International trade theory and policy*, McGraw-Hill Book Company, New York.

Chandler, A.D. (1962) *Strategy and structure: chapters in the history of the industrial enterprise*, MIT Press, Boston.

Chng, M.K. (1985) *ASEAN economic co-operation: The current status, Southeast Asian Affairs, Institute of Southeast Asian Studies*, Singapore pp. 31–53.

Coase, R.H. (1937) The nature of the firm, in R.H. Coase (ed), *The firm, the market, and the law,* University of Chicago Press, Chicago, pp. 33–55.

Cooper, C. and Massell, B. (1965) A new look at customs union theory, *The Economic Journal*, 75(300), pp. 742–747.

Corden, W. (1972) Economies of scale and customs union theory, *The Journal of Political Economy*, 80(3), pp. 465–475.

Cornett, L. and Caporaso, J.A. (1992) "And still it moves!" State interests and social forces in the European Community, in J. Rosenau and E.O. Czempiel (eds), *Governance without government: order and change in world politics*, Cambridge University Press, Cambridge, pp. 219–249.

Council of Europe (2024) Winston Churchill, speech delivered at the University of Zurich, 19 September 1946, https://rm.coe.int/16806981f3 (accessed: 05.04.2024).

Dahl, R. (1978) Pluralism revisited, *Comparative Politics*, 10(2), pp. 191–203.

Davis, L.E. and North, D.C. (1971) *Institutional change and American economic growth*, Cambridge University Press, Cambridge.

Davis, R.S. (1978) *The federal principle: A journey through time and quest of a meaning*, University of California Press, London.

De Melo, J. and Panagariya, A. (1993) Introduction, in J. De Melo, A. Panagariya (eds), *New dimensions in regional integration*, Cambridge University Press, Cambridge.

Demas, W.G. (1965) *The economics of development in small countries with special reference to the Caribbean*, McGill University Press, Montreal.

Dent, C.M. (2002) Introduction: Northeast Asia – a region in search of regionalism, in C.M. Dent, and D.W.F. Huang (eds), *Northeast Asian Regionalism. Learning from the European Experience*, Routledge, New York.

Dent, Ch .M. (2017) *East Asian integration towards an east asian economic community*, ADBI Working Paper Series, 665, Asian Development Bank Institute (ADBI).

Deutsch, K.W. (1953) *Nationalism and social communication: An inquiry into foundations of nationality*, MIT Press, Cambridge.

Deutsch, K.W. (1954) *Political community at the international level: Problems of definition and measurement*, Doubled & Company, Garden City.

Deutsch, K.W. (1963) *The nerves of government: Models of political communication and control*, Free Press, New York.

Deutsch, K.W. (1964) Communication theory and political integration, in P. Jacob, J. Toscano (eds), *The integration of political communities*, J.B. Lippincott Company, Philadelphia and New York.

Deutsch, K.W. (2003) Political community and the North Atlantic area, in B. Nelsen, A. Stubb (eds), *The European Union; Readings on the theory and Practice of European integration*, 3rd edition, Lynne Rienner Publishers, Boulder, pp. 122–124.

Deutsch, K.W., Burrell, S.A., Kann, R.A. and Lee, M. (1968) *Political community and the North Atlantic area: International organisation in the light of historical experience*, Princeton University Press, Princeton, NJ, pp. 5–6.

Dieter, H. (2020) End of the spaghetti bowl: RCEP does not create an Asia-Pacific trade bloc, *Asia Global*, 19 November.

Dieter, H. (2021) *RCEP-Countries create Asia-Pacific free trade zone: Trade facilitation but no integrated bloc*, SWP Comments 3/2021, Stiftung Wissenschaft und Politik (SWP), German Institute for International and Security Affairs.

Dosch, J. and Dent, C.M. (2012) *The Asia Pacific, regionalism and the global system*, Edward Elgar Publishing, Cheltenham.

Dosenrode, S. (2010) Federalism Theory and Neo-functionalism: Elements for an analytical framework, *Perspectives on Federalism*, 2(3), pp. 1–28.

Dosenrode, S. (2018) *Federalism as a theory of regional integration*, Oxford Research Encyclopaedia, Oxford University Press, Oxford, pp. 1–28.

EAVG (2001) Towards an East Asian community; Region of peace, prosperity and progress, East Asia Vision Group (EAVG) Report, 31 October.

EAVG (2012) Report of the East Asia Vision Group II (EAVG II), 1 November.

Eisenhardt, K.M. (1989) Agency theory: An assessment and review. *The Academy of Management Review*, 14(1), pp. 57–74.

El-Agra, A.M. (1988) *International economic integration*, Macmillan, London.

El-Agraa, A.M. (1983) *The theory of international trade*, St. Martin's Press, New York.

Elkan, P.G. (1975) Measuring the impact of economic integration among developing countries, *Journal of Common Market Studies*, 14(1), pp. 56–68.

Etzioni, A. (1965) *Political unification: A comparative study of leaders and forces*, Holt Rereliart and Winston, New York.

European Commission (2021). *Trade policy review; an open sustainable and assertive trade policy*, Publications Office of the European Union, Luxembourg.

Fernandez, R. (1997) *Returns to regionalism: An evaluation of non-traditional gains from regional trade agreements*, World Bank Policy Research Working Paper no.1816, World Bank, Washington, DC.

Ferrantino, M.J, Maliszewska, M. and Taran, S. (2020) *Actual and potential trade agreements in the Asia-Pacific: Estimated effects*, Policy Research Working Paper, 9496, World Bank.

Fligstein, N. and Stone Sweet, A. (2001) Constructing polities and market: An institutionalist account of European integration, *American Journal of Sociology*,107(5), pp. 1206–1243.

Gabriel, S. and Scharping, R. (2022) Europa macht sich zum Maß aller Dinge – und vergrätzt so wichtige Handelspartner, Handelsblatt, 26 January.

Gaedicke, H. and Eynern, G. (1933) *Die produktionswirtschaftliche Integration Europad: Eine Untersuchung über die Aussenhandelsverflechtung der europäischen Länder*, Junker and Dünnhaupt, Berlin.

Galanter, M. (1981) Justice in many rooms: Courts, private ordering, and indigenous law, *Journal of Legal Pluralism*, 19, pp. 1–47.

Gardner, L.C. (1970) *Architects of illusion: Men and ideas in American foreign policy 1941-1949*, Quadrangle, Chicago.

Gehrels, F. (1956) Customs union from a single-country viewpoint, *The Review of Economic Studies*, 24(1), pp. 61–64.

George, S. (1985) *Politics and policy in the European Community*, Clarendon Press, Oxford.

George, S. (1994) *Supranational actors and domestic politics: Integration theory reconsidered in the light of the Single European Act and Maastricht*, University of Sheffield, Sheffield.

Greif, A. (2006) *Institutions and the path to the modern economy: Lessons from medieval trade*, Cambridge University Press, Cambridge.

Haas, E.B (1958) *The uniting of Europe; Political, social and economic forces* 1950-1957, 1st edition, Stanford University Press, Stanford, CA.

Haas, E.B. (1960) *Consensus formation of the Council of Europe*, University of California Press, Berkeley.

Haas, E.B. (1961) International integration: The European and the universal process, *International Organisation*, 15(3), pp. 366–392.

Haas, E.B. (1964) *Beyond the nation state: Functionalism and international organisation*, Stanford University Press, Stanford, CA.

Haas, E.B. (1964) Technocracy, pluralism, and the new Europe, in S. Graubard (ed), *A new Europe?*, Hougton Mifflin, Boston, pp. 62–88.

Haas, E.B. (1967) The "uniting of Europe" and the "uniting of Latin America", *Journal of Common Market Studies,* 5(2), pp. 315–343.

Haas, E.B. (1970) The study of regional integration: Reflections on the joy and anguish of pretheorising, *International Organisation*, 24(4), pp. 607–646.

Haas, E.B. (1976) Turbulent fields in the theory of regional integration, *International Organisation*, 30(2), pp. 173–212.

Haas, E.B. (2001) Does constructivism subsume neofunctionalism? in T. Christiansen, K.E. Jørgensen and A. Wiener (eds), *The social construction of Europe*, Sage, London.

Haas, E.B. (2004) *The uniting of Europe: Politics, social and economic forces, 1950-1957*, 3rd edition, University of Notre Dame Press, Notre Dame.

Haggard, S. (1993) Comment, in J. Frankel and M. Kahler (eds), *Regionalism and rivarly: Japan and the United States in Pacific Asia*, The University of Chicago Press, Chicago, IL, pp. 48–52.

Haliżak, E. (1999) *Stosunki międzynarodowe w regionie Azji i Pacyfiku* [International relations in the Asia-Pacific region], Wydawnictwo Naukowe Scholar, Warsaw.

Hall, P.A. and Soskice, D. (2001) *Varieties of capitalism: The institutional foundations of comparative advantage*. Oxford University Press, Oxford.

Hallett, A.H. and Primo Braga, C.A. (1994) *The new regionalism and the threat of protectionism*, Policy Research Working Paper 1349, The World Bank.

Hallstein, W. (1962) *United Europe. Challenge and opportunity*, Harvard University Press, Cambridge.

Hansen, L. (1997) Nation-building on the Balkan border, *Alternatives*, 21, pp. 473–496.

Hart, O.D. and Moore, J. (1990) Property rights and the nature of the firm, *Journal of Political Economy*, 98, pp. 1119–1158.

Hayek, F.A. (1939) Economic conditions of inter-state federalism, *The New Commonwealth Quarterly*, 5(2), pp. 131–149.

Hayek, F.A. (1937) Economics and knowledge, *Economica*, 4(13), pp. 33–54.

Hayek, F.A. (1945) The use of knowledge in society, *The American Economic Review*, 35(4), pp. 519–530.

Heckscher, E. (1935) *Merkantilismen*, Norstedt and Söners, Stockholm 1931; English edition: E. Heckscher, *Mercantilism*, authorised translation by M. Shapiro, George Allen & Unwin, London.

Heilperin, H. (1957) Freer trade and social welfare. Some marginal comments on the "Ohlin Report", *International Labour Review*, 75(2), pp. 173–192.

Hettne, B. and Inotai A. (1994) *The new regionalism: implications for global development international security*, UNU/WIDER, Helsinki.

Hilgerdt, F. (1942) *The network of world trade*, Economic Intelligence Service, League of Nations, Geneva.

Hilpert, H.G. (2022) *Sea change in EU trade policy: opportunities for diversification in the Indo-Pacific*, (SWP Comment, 59/2022), Stiftung Wissenschaft und Politik -SWP- Deutsches Institut für Internationale Politik und Sicherheit, Berlin.

Hirschman, A. (1971) *A bias for hope: Essays on development and Latin America*, Yale University Press, New Haven and London.

Hodgson, G.M. (1996) *Institutional economic theory: The old versus the new*, in G.M. Hodgson (ed), *After Marx and Straffa: Essays in political economy*, St. Martin's Press, New York, pp. 194–213.

Hoffman, S. (1966) Obstinate or obsolete? The fate of the nation-state and the case of Western Europe, *Daedalus*, 95, pp. 862–915.

Hofstadter, R. and Hofstadter, B.K. (eds) (1982) *Great issues in American history, vol. III: From reconstruction to the present day, 1864-1981*, rev. edition, Vintage, New York.

Hoppe, H.-H. (2007) *Democracy the god that failed: The economics and politics of monarchy, democracy, and natural order*, Transaction Publishers, New Brunswick and London.

https://www.cvce.eu/en/obj/statement_by_paul_hoffman_at_the_75th_oeec_council_meeting_31_october_1949-en-840d9b55-4d17-4c33-8b09-7ea547b85b40.html (accessed: 05.04.2024).

Inotai, A. (1991) *Regional integration among developing countries, revisited*, Policy, Research, and External Affairs Working Paper no. 643, World Bank, Washington, DC.

Intan, R. (2020) What RCEP can tell us about geopolitics in Asia, The Interpreter, 1 December, https://www.lowyinstitute.org/the-interpreter/what-rcep-can-tell-us-about-geopolitics-asia (accessed: 13.07.2024).

Jensen, M.C. and Meckling, W. (1976) Theory of the firm: Managerial behavior, agency costs, and ownership structure, *Journal of Financial Economics*, 3, pp. 305–360.

Johnson, H. (1962) *Money, trade and economic growth. Survey lectures on economic theory*, Routledge, London.

Johnson, H. (1975) A note on welfare-increasing trade diversion, *The Canadian Journal of Economics*, 8(1), pp.117–123.

Kant, I. (1917) *Perpetual peace: A philosophical essay*, George Allen & Unwin Ltd, London, The Macmillan Company, New York.

Kahnert, F., Richards, P., Stoutjesdijk, E. and Thomopoulos, P. (1969) *Economic integration among developing countries*, Development Centre of the OECD, Paris.

Katzenstein, P.J. (2005) *A world of regions: Asia and the Europe in the American Imperium*, Cornwell University Press, Ithaca.

Kemp, M. (1969) *The pure theory of international trade and investment*, Prentice-Hall, London.

Kemp, M. and Wan, H. (1976) An elementary proposition concerning the formation of customs unions, *Journal of International Economics*, 6, pp. 95–97.

Kennan, J. and Riezman, R. (1990) Optimal tariff equilibria with customs unions, *Canadian Journal of Economics*, 90, pp. 70–78.

Keohane, R. (1984) *After hegemony. Cooperation and discord in the world political economy*, Princeton University Press, Princeton, NJ.

Keohane, R. and Hoffmann, S. (1991) *The new European Community: Decision-making and institutional change*, Westview, Boulder and Oxford.

Keohane, R. and Nye, J. (1975) *International interdependence and integration*, in F. Greenstein, N. Polsby (eds), *Handbook of political science*, Addison-Wesley, Reading, MA, pp. 363–377.

Keohane, R.O. (1989) Neoliberal institutionalism: A perspective on world politics, in R.O. Kehane (ed.), *International institutions and state power: Esseys in international relations theory*, 1st edition, Routledge, New York.

Kim, J. and Mahoney, J.T. (2005) Property rights theory, transaction costs theory, and agency theory: An organizational economics approach to strategic management, *Managerial and Decision Economics*, 26(4), pp. 223–242.

Kindleberger, C. (1963) European economic integration and the development of a single financial center for long term capital, *Weltwissenschaftliches Archiv*, 2, pp. 190–192.

King, P. (1982) *Federalism and federation*, Johns Hopkins University Press, Baltimore.

Kinsky, F. (1979) Personalism and federalism, *The Journal of Federalism*, 9(4), pp. 131–156.

Klabbers, J. (2009) *An introduction to international law*, 2nd edition, Cambridge University Press, Cambridge.

Klein, P.G. (2000) *New institutional economics in encyclopedia of law and economics*, Edward Elgar, Cheltenham, pp. 456–489.

Kojima, K. (2000) The "flying geese" model of Asian economic development: origin, theoretical extensions, and regional policy implications, *Journal of Asian Economics*, 1, pp. 375–340.

Krauss, M. (1972) Recent developments in customs union theory: An interpretive survey, *Journal of Economic Literature*, 10(2), pp.413–436.

Kreinin, M. (1964) On the dynamic effects of a customs union, *The Journal of Political Economy*, 72(2), pp. 193–195.

Krissoff, B. and Sharples, J. (1993) Preferential trading arrangements in Western Hemisphere countries, *Agricultural and Resource Economics Review*, 22 (1), pp. 1–11.

Kuwayama, M. (1999). *Open regionalism in Asia Pacific and Latin America: a survey of the literature*, International Trade and Development Finance Division, Santiago.

Lawrence, R. (1997) *Preferential trading arrangements: The traditional and the new*, in A. Galal and B. Hoekman (eds), *Regional partners in global markets: Limits and possibilities of the Euro-Med* agreements, Center for Economic Policy Research (CEPR) and the Egyptian Center for Economic Studies (ECES).

Lee, K. (2020) Varieties of capitalism and re-thinking the East Asian model of economic growth after the COVID-19: Rebalancing shareholder and stakeholder capitalism, *Seoul Journal of Economics*, 33(4), pp. 487–504.

Lee, K. and Shin, H. (2021) Varieties of capitalism and East Asia: Long-term evolution, structural change, and the end of East Asian capitalism, *Structural Change and Economic Dynamics*, 56, pp. 431–437.

Lindberg, L. (1963) *The political dynamics of European economic integration*, Stanford University Press, Stanford, CA.

Lindberg, L. and Scheingold, S. (1970) *Europe's would be polity: Patterns of change in the European Community*, Prentice Hall, Englewood Cliffs.

Lindberg, L. and Scheingold, S. (eds) (1971), *Regional integration; Theory and research*, Harvard University Press, Cambridge, MA.

Lindberg, L.N. (1967) The European Community as a political system, *Journal of Common Market Studies*, 5(4), pp. 344–387.

Lipsey R.G. (1957) The theory of customs union: Trade diversion and welfare, *Economica*, 24(93), pp. 40–46.

Lipsey, R.G. (1960) The theory of customs unions: A general survey, *The Economic Journal*, 70(279), pp. 496–513.

Lipsey, R.G. (1970) *The theory of custom unions: A general equilibrium analysis*, Weidenfeld and Nicholson, London.

Lipsey, R.G. (1991) The case for trilateralism, in S. Globerman (ed), *Continental accord: North American economic integration*, The Fraser Institute, Vancouver, pp. 89–124.

Lloyd, P. (1982) A 3x3 theory of customs unions, *Journal of International Economics*,12, pp. 41–63.

Longi, S. and Nijkamp, P. (2007) *Economic integration and labour markets: Ways forward*, in G. Korres (ed), *Regionalisation, growth and economic integration*, Physica-Verlag, Heidelberg, pp. 3–24.

Machlup, F. (1977) *A history of thought on economic integration*, The Macmillan Press Ltd, London and Basingstoke.

Mahoney, J and Thelen, K. (2012) *Explaining institutional change: Ambiguity, agency, and power*, Cambridge University Press, Cambridge.

Makower, H. and Morton, G. (1953) A contribution towards a theory of customs unions, *The Economic Journal*, 63(249), pp. 33–49.

Mally, G. (1973) *The European Community in perspective – the new Europe, the United States and world*, Lexington Books, Lexington.

Mansfield E.D and Solingen, E. (2010) Regionalism, *Annual Review of Political Science*, 13(1), pp. 145–163.

March, J., Simon, H. and Guetzkow, H. (1958) *Organisations*, John Wiley and Sons, Inc., New York; Chapman and Hall, Ltd, London.

Marinov, E. (2014) Economic integration theories and the developing countries, *Munich Personal RePEc Archive*, September.

Marinov, V. (1999) *Regional economic integration*, PH Stopanstvo, Sofia.

Marjolin, R. (1955) *Europe and United States in the world economy*, Duke University Press, Durham.

Meade, J. (1955) *The theory of customs unions*, North-Holland, Amsterdam.

Meade, J. (1956) The theory of customs unions, *The Economic Journal*, 66(262), pp. 337–339.

Meier, G.M. (1960) Effects of a customs union on economic development, *Social and Economic Studies*, March.

Mikesell, R.F. (1965) *The theory of common markets as applied to regional arrangements among developing countries*, in R. Harrod, D. Hague (eds), *International trade theory in a developing world*, St. Martin's Press, New York.

Miklaszewski, S. (1984) Uwagi o stanie teorii integracji w literaturze zachodniej [Remarks on the state of the integration theory in Western literature], *Folia Economica Cracoviensia*, XXVII, pp. 183–193.

Miklaszewski, S. (1991) Mechanizm regionalnej integracji gospodarczej w teorii i praktyce Europejskiej Wspólnoty Gospodarczej [The mechanism of regional economic integration in the theory and practice of European Economic Community], *Zeszyty Naukowe/Akademia Ekonomiczna w Krakowie*, 99.

Minghui, S. (2017) Lifting global free trade from the 'noodle bowl', *East Asia Forum*, 9 March, https://eastasiaforum.org/2017/03/09/lifting-global-free-trade-from-the-noodle-bowl/ (accessed: 13.07.2024).

Misala, J. (2005) *Wymiana międzynarodowa i gospodarka światowa; Teoria i mechanizmy funkcjonowania [International exchange and world economy: the theory and mechanisms of functioning]*, Szkoła Główna Handlowa, Warsaw.

Mistry, P.S. (1995) *Open regionalism: stepping stone or millstone toward an improved multilateral system?* in J.J. Teunissen (ed), *Regionalism and the global economy: the case of Latin America and the Caribbean*, FONDAD, The Hague.

Mitrany, D. (1943) *A working peace system: An argument for the functional development of international organisation*, Royal Institute of International Affairs, London.

Mitrany, D. (1966) The prospects of integration: Federal or functional, *Journal of Common Market Studies*, 4(2), pp. 119–149.

Mitrany, D. (1975) *The functional theory of politics*, Macmillan, London.

Molle, W. (2001) *The economics of European integration: Theory, practice, policy*, 4th edition, Ashgate, London.

Moore, J.D. (2018) *Varieties Of Capitalism in Southeast Asia*, Palgrave Macmillan, Cham.

Moravcsik, A. (1993) Preferences and power in the European Community: A liberal intergovernmental approach, *Journal of Common Market Studies*, 31(4), pp. 475–476.

Moravcsik, A. (1998) *The choice for Europe. Social purpose and state power from Messina to Maastricht*, Cornell University Press, Ithaca.

Moravcsik, A. (2008) The new liberalism, in C. Reus-Smit, D. Snidal (eds), *The Oxford handbook of international relations*, Oxford University Press, Oxford, pp. 234–254.

Moravcsik, A. and Schimmelfenning, F. (2009) *Liberal intergovernmentalism*, in A. Wiener and T. Diez, *European integration theory*, 2nd edition, Oxford University Press, Oxford.

Munakata, N. (2003) *The impact of the rise of China and regional economic integration in Asia – a Japanese perspective*, Testiomony before the US-China Economic and Security Commission Hearing on China's Growth as a Regional Power: Impacts and Implications, 4 December.

Munakata, N. (2004) *Regionalisation and Regionalism: The process of mutual interaction*, RIETI Discussion Paper Series 04-E-006.

Munakata, N. (2006) *Transforming East Asia: the evolution of regional economic integration*, Brookings Institution Press, Washington DC.

Myrdal, G. (1956) *Development and underdevelopment: A note on the mechanism of national and international economic inequality*, National Bank of Egypt, Cairo.

Nee, V. (1998) Sources of the new institutionalism, in M.C. Brinton and V. Nee (eds), *The new institutionalism in sociology*, Russell Sage Foundation, New York, pp. 1–16.

New Zealand Foreign Affairs and Trade (2024) Comprehensive and Progressive Agreement for Trans-Pacific Partnership texts, https://www.mfat.govt.nz/en/trade/free-trade-agreements/free-trade-agreements-in-force/cptpp/comprehensive-and-progressive-agreement-for-trans-pacific-partnership-text-and-resources/#bookmark0 (accessed: 05.04.2024).

Nicita, A. (2021) *An assessment of the Regional Comprehensive Economic Partnership (RCEP) tariff concessions*, UNCTAD Research Papers, 73, United Nations Conference on Trade and Development (UNCTAD), Geneva.

Nicolas, F. (2010) De facto and de jure regional economic integration in East Asia: How do they interact, *The Singapore Economic Review*, 55(1), pp. 7–25.

Niemann, A.L. and Schmitter, P.C. (2009) *Neofunctionalism*, in A. Wiener and T. Diez, *European integration theory*, 2nd edition, Oxford University Press, Oxford.

North, D. (1990) *Institutions, institutional change and economic performance*, Cambridge University Press, Cambridge.

Nye, J. (1965) *Pan-Africanism and East African Federation*, Harvard University Press, Cambridge, MA.

Nye, J.S. (1971) *Peace in parts*, Little Brown, Boston.

Nye, J.S. (1968) *International regionalism*, Little Brown and Co, Boston.

OECD (2024) The "Marshall Plan" speech at Harvard University, 5 June 1947, https://www.oecd.org/general/themarshallplanspeechatharvarduniversity5june1947.htm (accessed: 05.04.2024).

Okita, S. (1992) Japan's role in Asia-Pacific cooperation, *The Annals of the American Academy of Political and Social Science*, 513, pp. 25–37.

Online Etymology Dictionary (2024), https://www.etymonline.com/ (accessed: 05.04.2024).

Panusheff, E. (2003) *Economic integration in the European Union*, PH Nekst, Sofia.

Parada, J.J. (2005) Original institutional economics and new institutional economics: Revisiting the bridges (or the divide), *Revista de Economía Institucional*, 5(8), pp. 92–116.

Park, C.-Y, Petri P.A. and Plummer, M.G. (2021) *Economic implications of the regional comprehensive economic partnership for Asia and the Pacific*, ABD Economics Working Paper Series no. 639, Asian Development Bank.

Park, I. (2022) *Comparison of the Regional Comprehensive Economic Partnership and other free trade agreements*, in F. Kimura, S. Thangavelu and D. Narjoko (eds), *Regional comprehensive economic partnership: implications, challenges, and future growth of East Asia, ASEAN* Economic Research Institute for ASEAN and East Asia (ERIA), Jakarta, pp. 45–82.

Pascha, W. (2004) *Economic integration in East Asia and Europe – A comparison*, Duisburger Arbeitspapiere zur Ostasienwirtschaft, 68/2004.

Pelkmans, J. (2001) *European integration, methods and economics analysis*, 2nd edition, Pearson, Harlow.

Pempel T.J. (ed.) (2005) *Remapping East Asia. The construction of the region*, Cornell University Press, Ithaca.

Pentland, C. (1973) *International theory and European integration*, Faber and Faber, London.

Peters, B.G. (1999) *Institutional theory in political science: The 'new institutionalism'*, Pinter, London.

Petri P.A. and Plummer, M.G. (2020a) RCEP: A new trade agreement that will shape global economics and politics, Brookings, November 16, https://www.brookings.edu/articles/rcep-a-new-trade-agreement-that-will-shape-global-economics-and-politics/ (accessed: 13.07.2024).

Petri, P.A. and Plummer, M.G. (2020b) *East Asia decouples from the United States: Trade war, COVID-19, and East Asia's new trade blocs,* PIIE Working Paper, 20(9), Peterson Institute for International Economics, (PIIE).

Philip, F. (1957) Social aspects of European economic co-operation, *International Labour Review*, 76(3), pp. 244–256.

Pierson, P. (1996) The path to European integration: A historical institutionalist analysis, *Comparative Political Studies*, 29(2), pp. 123–163.

Politico (2020) 5 Reasons the Asia-Pacific trade deal matters for Europe, A mega deal between 15 Asian economies triggers headaches for Brussels', *Politico*, 23 November.

Pollack, M. (2001) International relations theory and European integration, *Journal of Common Market Studies*, 39(2), pp. 221–244.

Pomfret, R. (1997) *The economics of regional trading arrangements*, Clarendon Press, Oxford.

Pornjantuek, L., Romprasert, S. and Trivedi, A., (2020) Effects of China trade war on Singapore economy in 2020, *Social Science Asia*, 8(1), pp. 75–88.

Price, H.B. (1955) *The Marshall Plan and its meaning*, Cornell University Press, Ithaca.

Próchniak, M. and Suska, M. (2023) *Realna konwergencja w krajach Azji Wschodniej a instytucjonalizacja regionalnej współpracy i integracji gospodarczej [Real convergence in East Asia's countries and the institutionalisation of regional cooperation and economic integration*, in D. Kopycińska and J. Korpysa (eds), *Współczesne Problemy Gospodarowania [Contemporary issues of the economy],* Fundacja Centrum Badań Socjologicznych, Szczecin, pp. 11–25.

Puchala, D.J. (1966) *European political integration: Progress and prospects*, Yale University Political Science Research Library, New Haven.

Puchala, D.J. (1972) Of blind men, elephants and international integration, *Journal of Common Market Studies*, 10(3), pp. 267–284.

Quimba, F.M.A. and Barral, M.A. (2019) *The evolution of APEC and its role in the Philippine trade and investment*, Discussion Paper Series no. 2019, Philippine Institute for Development Studies.

Rath, S. (1978) Federalism: A conceptual analysis, *The Indian Journal of Political Science*, 39(4), pp. 573–586.

Riezman, R. (1979) A 3x3 model of customs unions, *Journal of International Economics*, 9(3), pp. 341–354.

Riezman, R. (1985) Customs unions and the core, *Journal of International Economics*, 19(3-4), pp. 355–365.

Riezman, R. (1999) Can bilateral agreements help introduce free trade?, *Canadian Journal of Economics*, 32, pp. 751–766.

Robson, P. (1987) *The economics of international integration*, Allen & Unwin Ltd, London.

Roche, J.J. (1999) *Relations Internationales*, LGDJ, Paris.

Roemheld, L. (1990) *Integral federalism: Model for Europe - a way towards a personal group society- historical development, philosophy, state, economy, society*, Peter Lang, Frankfurt/M., Bern, New York, Paris

Rometsch, D. and Wessels, W. (1996) *The European Union and member states: Towards institutional fusion?* Manchester University Press, Manchester.

Röpke, W. (1957) *Integration und Desintegration der internationalen Wirtschaft*, in *Wirtschaftsfragen der freien Welt*, Erhard-Festschrift, Frankfurt.

Röpke, W. (1959) *International order and economic integration,* D. Reidel Publishing Company, Dordrecht.

Rueda-Junquera, F. (2006) *European integration model: Lessons for the Central American common market*, Jean Monnet/Robert Shuman Paper Series, 6(4), University of Miami, Coral Gables, FL.

Ruggie, J.G. (1998) *Constructing the World Policy: Essays on International Institutionalisation*, Routledge, London.

Sakamoto, J. (1969) Industrial development and integration of underdeveloped countries, *Journal of Common Market Studies*, 7(4), pp. 283–304.

Sannwald, R. and Stohler, J (1969) *Economic integration: Theoretical assumptions and consequences of European unification*, Greenwood Press, Westport, CT.

Schiff M. and Winters, L. (1998) Dynamics and politics in regional integration arrangements: An introduction, *The World Bank Economic Review*, 12(2), pp.177–195.

Schmitter, P.C. (1969) Three neo-functional hypotheses about international integration, *International Organisation*, 23, pp. 562–564.

Schmitter, P.C. (1970) A revised theory of regional integration, International Organisation, 24(Autumn), pp. 836–868.

Schmitter, P.C. (1971) *A revised theory of regional integration*, in L. Lindberg and S. Scheingold (eds), *Regional integration: Theory and research*, Harvard University Press, Cambridge, MA, pp. 232–265.

Schmitter, P.C. (1996) *Imaging the future of the euro-polity with help of new concepts*, in G. Marks, F. Scharpf, and P. Schmitter et al. (eds), *Governance in the European Union*, Sage, London, pp. 121–150.

Schmitter, P.C. (1997) *The emerging Europolity and its impact on national systems of production*, in J. Rogers Hollingsworth, R, Boyer (eds), *Contemporary capitalism: The embeddedness of institutions*, Cambridge University Press, Cambridge, pp. 395–430.

Schmitter, P.C. (2004) *Neofunctionalism*, in A. Wiener and T. Diez (eds), *European integration theory*, 1st edition, Oxford University Press, Oxford, pp. 46–74.

Scitovsky, T. (1958) *Economic theory and Western European integration*, Stanford University Press, Stanford, CA.

Scott, A.J. (1999) *Regions and the world economy: The coming shape of global production, competition, and political order*, Oxford University Press, Oxford.

Scott, W.R. (2008) *Institutions and organisations: Ideas and interests*, 3rd edition, Sage Publications, Thousand Oaks, CA.

Scott, W.R. (2010) Reflections: the past and future research on institutions and institutional change, *Journal of Change Management*, 10(1), pp. 5–21.

Selznick, P. (1957) *Leadership in administration*, Harper & Row, New York.

Selznick, P (1959) Book review. Organizations. By James G. March and Herbert Simon. With the collaboration of Harold Guetzkow. *American Sociological Review*, 24, pp. 911–913.

Sewell, J.P. (1966) *Functionalism and world politics*, Princeton University Press, Princeton, NJ.

Sheer, A. (1981) A survey of the political economy of customs unions, *Law and Contemporary Problems*, 44(3), pp.33–53.

Simon, H. (1961) *Administrative behavior*, 2nd edition, Mc Millan, New York.

Soesastro, H. (2005) *The evolution of ASEAN+X free trade agreements: Implications for Canada*, CSIS Working Paper Series, WPE 089, February.

Soesastro, H. (2006) Regional integration in East Asia: Achievements and future prospects, *Asian Economic Policy Review*, 1(2), pp. 215–234.

Spire Research and Consulting (2024) Regional Comprehensive Economic Partnership (RCEP), https://www.spireresearch.com/regional-comprehensive-economic-partnership-rcep/ (accessed 13 July 2024).

Spraos, J. (1964) The condition for a trade-creating customs union, *The Economic Journal*, 74(293), pp.101–108.

Stone Sweet, A., Sandholtz, W. and Fligstein N. (eds) (2001) *The institutionalisation of Europe*, Oxford University Press, New York.

Suska M. (2022) *Poland and other EU members' trade relations with Asian economies*, in A.A. Ambroziak (ed.), *Poland in the European Union: Report 2022*, Szkoła Główna Handlowa w Warszawie, Warsaw, pp. 139–160.

Suska, M. (2023) Institutionalisation of economic integration and its impact on trade and growth: A new look at RCEP economies from East Asian perspective, in W. Mierzejewska and P. Dziurski (eds), *International business from East to West: Global risks and opportunities, Szkoła Główna Handlowa w Warszawie*, Warsaw, pp. 270–280.

Syadullah, M. and Ardiansyah, B.G. (2017) Cost benefit analysis the participation of Indonesia in Asia Region funds passport, *International Journal of Economics and Financial Issues, Econjournals*, 7(3), pp. 128–134.

Taylor, P. (1983) *The limits of European integration*, Croom Helm, London.

Thelen, K. (1999) Historical institutionalism in comparative politics, *Annual Review of Political Science*, 2, pp. 369–404.

Tinbergen, J. (1954) *International economic integration*, 2nd rev. edition, Elsevier, Brussels.

UN Comtrade Database (2022), https://comtradeplus.un.org/TradeFlow?Frequency=A&Flows=X&CommodityCodes=TOTAL&Partners=0&Reporters=all&period=2023&AggregateBy=none&BreakdownMode=plus (accessed: 13.07.2024).

UNCTAD (2007) *Trade and development report 2007: Regional cooperation for development*, UNCTAD/TDR/2007, United Nations, Geneva.

UNCTAD (2021). Key statistics and trends in trade policy, https://unctad.org/system/files/official-document/ditctab2022d2_en.pdf (accessed: 13.10.2023).

UNCTAD (2024) https://unctadstat.unctad.org/datacentre/dataviewer/US.TradeMerchTotal (accessed: 13.10.2023).

Urata, S. (2009) Institutionalization of regional economic integration in East, https://www.rieti.go.jp/en/events/09082801/pdf/29-1-1_Urata_Paper.pdf (accessed: 12.11.2023).

US Department of State (1998) Asia-Pacific economic cooperation (APEC), Bureau of East Asian and Pacific Affairs.

U.S. Department of State, October 26, https://1997-2001.state.gov/regions/eap/fs-apec_981026.html (accessed: 07.10.2024).

Viner, J. (1950) *The customs union issue*, Carnegie Endowment for International Peace, New York.

Visual Capitalist (2024) Mapped: The top exports in Asian countries, https://www.visualcapitalist.com/mapped-the-top-exports-in-asian-countries/ (accessed: 13.07.2024).

Webb, C. (1983) *Theoretical perspectives and problems*, in H. Wallace et al. (eds), *Policy-making in the European Community*, Wiley, Chichester, pp. 1–41.

Wessels, W. (1997) An ever closer fusion? A dynamic macropolitical view on integration processes, *Journal of Common Market Studies*, 35(2), pp. 267–299.

Wessels, W. (2005) The constitutional treaty: Three readings from a fusion perspective, *Journal of Common Market Studies*, 43(1), pp. 11–36.

Wiener, N. (1950) *The human use of human beings: Cybernetics and society*, Houghton Mifflin, Boston.

Williamson, O.E. (1975) *Markets and hierarchies: Analysis and antitrust implications*, Free Press, New York.

Williamson, O.E. (1985) *The economic institutions of capitalism*, The Free Press, New York.

Williamson, O.E. (1994) *Transaction cost economics and organization theory*, in N.J. Smelser and R. Swedberg (eds) *The Handbook of Economic Sociology*, 1st edition, Princeton University Press and Russell Sage Foundation, Princeton, NJ, pp. 77–107.

Wonnacott, R. (1990) *U.S. hub-and-spoke bilateral and the multilateral trading system*, C.D. House Institute, no. 23, Toronto.

Wooton, I. (1986) Preferential trading agreements: An investigation, *Journal of International Economics*, 21, pp. 81–97.

World Development Indicators (2024), https://databank.worldbank.org/source/world-development-indicators (accessed: 13.07.2024).

WTO (2024) Comprehensive and Progressive Agreement for Trans-Pacific Partnership (CPTPP) (goods and services), Report by the Secretariat, 26 August, https://web.wtocenter.org.tw/file/PageFile/401842/WTREG395-5.pdf (accessed: 20.09.2024).

WTO (2024) Regional Trade Agreements – GATT Article XXIV, https://www.wto.org/english/tratop_e/region_e/region_art24_e.htm (accessed: 08.04.2024).

Yang, T.H. and Huang, D.S. (2011) *Multinational corporations, FDI and the East Asian Economic Integration*, RIETI Discussion Paper Series 11-E-071, Tokyo.

Yoshimatsu, H. (2002) Preferences, interests and regional integration: The development of the ASEAN industrial cooperation arrangement, *Review of International Political Economy*, 9(1), pp. 123–149.

Index

Note: **Bold** numbers refer to tables and page numbers followed by "n" denote endnotes.

Printed and bound by CPI Group (UK) Ltd, Croydon, CR0 4YY
12/11/2024
01787828-0002